The Great G.
Chronicles

Letting Go

Beth Anne Grimm

Calling him Great Grandpa
was the only way I could love him.

THE GREAT GRANDPA CHRONICLES

A DAUGHTER'S JOURNEY
FROM
AMBIVALENCE TO ACCEPTANCE

BY BETH GRIMM

WHY, YOU MIGHT ASK, IS THIS BOOK CALLED
THE GREAT GRANDPA CHRONICLES
WHEN IT IS ABOUT ME AND MY FATHER?

BECAUSE IT'S THE ONLY WAY
I COULD LOVE HIM.

The Great Grandpa Chronicles
Letting Go
All Rights Reserved.
Copyright © 2021 Beth Anne Grimm
v3.0

The opinions expressed in this manuscript are solely the opinions of the author and do not represent the opinions or thoughts of the publisher. The author has represented and warranted full ownership and/or legal right to publish all the materials in this book.

This book may not be reproduced, transmitted, or stored in whole or in part by any means, including graphic, electronic, or mechanical without the express written consent of the publisher except in the case of brief quotations embodied in critical articles and reviews.

Outskirts Press, Inc.
http://www.outskirtspress.com

ISBN: 978-1-9772-3285-4

Cover Photo © 2021 Beth Anne Grimm. All rights reserved - used with permission.

Outskirts Press and the "OP" logo are trademarks belonging to Outskirts Press, Inc.

PRINTED IN THE UNITED STATES OF AMERICA

DEDICATION

Nathaniel, Noah, Kyla, Emilie, and Elijah inspired me to write these stories. The youngest of my grandchildren were just babies when the fifth-year birthday party reunions began. Three generations gathered every five years at Great Grandpa's home, late in his life, not just to acknowledge his birthday, but to be with each other.

And so it is that "The Old Farm Boy", as Great Grandpa called himself, became a catalyst. His wanting to be celebrated, which brought us all together, and my resistance, which might have otherwise kept us at arms' length to the very end, made him my most peculiar muse.

I dedicate this book to my grandchildren because they gave me these stories to write. In recounting experiences, changes in family dynamics, and seeing my father through their untainted lenses as he became Great Grandpa, I was able to make the difficult climb from one side of the Mt. Everest of relationship challenges to the other.

We can do anything we put our minds to. That is and always will be the Grimm-Maas tradition and belief.

CONTENTS

A window shade came down between us.

INTRODUCTION

A comedian once said, "If there are two or more people in a family, it's dysfunctional."

Some might argue with that, but not me.

At the time I began to write the stories in this book, I didn't like my father very much. Acting as a dutiful daughter, I tried many different things to please him, but most fell flat. Not because they weren't worthy attempts, but because he lacked sufficient compassion to appreciate the efforts.

Logically, I knew what his problem was. He was a product of his life and time, raised by a poor, hard-worn Iowa farmer who ruled the house with an iron-fist, quick with the belt, and a soft spoken marshmallow bunny of a mother who would never question or challenge her husband. There was no role model to teach him appreciation for the women in his life.

And I knew what my problem was: I was far from a marshmallow bunny, but I needed him to love me anyway. Logic doesn't really help when the heart is at stake.

My father was not an empathetic man. Once he was out from under the constraints of farm life and on his way to success, he cruised life at the surface, always seeing himself in the best light, never admitting fault. Meanwhile, I tumbled around in emotions, sometimes gasping for air.

In my teens, I became angry and frustrated with my father for moving on, losing interest in his family, leaving my mother for another woman. A window shade came down between us, affecting the way I perceived him my whole life.

As an adult, I remained guarded. When I started writing personal essays about my father in my fifties, all I could produce were cathartic, whiny pages peppered with frustration and regrets. At some point, I realized the rubbish on the pages might be helping me vent, but it wasn't worth sharing with anyone else, and that left me alone in my grief.

When he reached old age and could not continue to do the things he loved, he began to call on me to organize celebratory parties for "the Old Farm Boy." That was a nickname he had given himself to emphasize the breadth of his rise from a poor Iowa farm to his beautiful life. Every five years, he'd remind me it was time, and expect me to arrange a party for him. He was lucky I rose to the occasion. As it turned out, so was I.

I'd gather my scattered chicks from opposite ends of the country for a long weekend in Arkansas. On the one hand, I detested his insistence we all gather around to celebrate him but on the other, I loved the idea of bringing my family together. While ostensibly celebrating my father, I could in fact honor myself.

Searching desperately for a turning point in my writing, I took a closer look, and noticed that at these five-year events, he was so ridiculously predictable in his attempts to control everyone and everything, it was humorous. I wanted to enjoy writing, so I began memorializing interactions and events at the reunions, taking well-earned potshots in the process. This felt redemptive.

The five-year birthday parties turned out to be my saving grace in this father-daughter relationship. Thanks to these reunions, and my father's evolution into Great Grandpa, I got the chance to perceive him through the innocent eyes of my grandchildren. The window shade slid up a few degrees with each new story.

And the stories in this book provide a backdrop to "the Old Farm Boy" that my grandchildren won't get from anyone else.

For me, the long journey from ambivalence to acceptance became a rite of passage in my most challenging familial relationship. Had I caught on at a younger age, I might have seen him as the damaged specimen worth studying that he was, rather than a vexing disappointment.

But that would have been a different journey. As it happened, I did not begin to understand myself until I fully considered who my father was. As he morphed from vexing father into quirky Great Grandpa, I was also aging, and my vision was softening. This evolution saved me from considerable grief and pain when he died. Without guilt, antipathy, or residual angst, I had completed my journey from ambivalence to acceptance. A welcome warmth swathed me the moment he passed away on December 12, 2019.

Thanks to the stories in this book, the window shade has rolled all the way up into itself. My view is clear and the corner of my heart he lives in is healed.

I hope this book will serve others who have suffered from emotional distancing or a lack of equality and respect in a relationship by seeing how a shift in perspective and introspection can make a difference.

L-R back. Greig, Keo, Kristin, Mark, Barbara, Me, Nathaniel
L-R Middle. Jason, Megan, Marcia, Jill, Esther, Dad, Ryan
L-R Front Elijah, Lincoln, Emilie, Dillon, Kyla, Noah

CAST OF CHARACTERS

It helps to know whose who. We are a family connected by blood, marriage, and divorce.

Me, My Parents and Siblings

Me, Beth Grimm
My Dad / Great Grandpa, William K Maas Sr. (pronounced Moss)
William K Maas Jr., my brother,
Barbara Mortier, my sister, also referred to as Aunt Barbara

My Children by Birth and Marriage

Ryan Grimm, my son
Ryan's wife, Jill, my daughter-in-law
Ryan's eldest son Nathaniel (from first marriage)
Ryan's daughter Emilie (with mother, Jill)
Ryan's youngest son Elijah (with mother, Jill)

Kristin Springer, my daughter
Kristin's husband Keo, my son-in-law
Their children, son Noah and daughter Kyla

Extended Family Members

Marge, My step-mother
Lynn, her daughter
Lane, her son

Lorena, Married to My step-brother Lane
Sven and Alex, their two boys

Mark, Barbara's husband, also called Uncle Mark

My Former Husband and his family

Greig Grimm, my former husband
Marcia Grimm, his current wife
Megan, their daughter
Jason, their son-in-law
And their two young sons Dillon and Lincoln

And Others

Marlen Soldana, long-time caregiver, who was close to
Great Grandpa until the day he died, his most steady
care-giver of several years

June Sullens, long-time secretary/office manager and
friend, like family for sixty years

Elmer, Karoake buddy, friend, and helper Joyce, Elmer's
wife, agency's designated caregiver

Colette, short-term caregiver, lasting less than a week

Esther, long-time friend and occasional companion.
Regular Saturday afternoon Gin Rummy challenger

PART 1

DAD BEING DAD

When I was six, he seemed like a good one.

When I was six, my father looked like a good one. Nothing seemed complicated when I was very young. But then, in my teens, I was seriously affected by my father's distancing from the family. With a yearning for the right kind of male attention, at twenty I married a man who appeared in the beginning to be my knight-in-shining- armor. However, after having kids, rather than supporting my aspirations to get a college education like he had accomplished with my full support, I found that he shared one of my father's most unbearable traits – a belief that his happiness was more important than mine. The marriage didn't last.

By the time I reached sixty, I still hadn't reconciled my feelings about my father. I was just too busy to worry about it amidst the crazy struggles as a single mother. I raised two kids while working and going to night law school. It was hard work but a good life. While running a satisfying, productive law practice, I also spent a lot of time with my kids and their kids. And thirty years flew by without fretting too much about my father or the men who crossed my path.

When I got off that roller coaster, a different life was waiting. A writing life. It began with the whiny, cathartic essays about my father. As it happened, the spiteful scribbled rants served as a dose of antibiotics to dissipate the effects of the viral resentment that lived in my system for more than thirty years. During this process I stumbled onto the truth, that I was ambivalent toward him. And I didn't like it.

I had to rip at deep scars in order to change. It would've been easier to jump off a bridge. But once I began to write something I thought might be worth sharing, the real healing began. I just didn't know it at the time.

Beautiful Bella Vista Resort in the heart of the Ozarks.

DAD AND THE TIMESHARE TOUR

Young Dave-with-the-drawl parked about a football field away from the runway. No one got out. We just sat there, motor running, …. But then … we heard a whirrrrrrr ….

The Tour Group.

There's me. At twenty, I was married. This pleased my father, as he did not really consider a woman complete unless she had a man. I was twenty-one in 1970, when we took this tour.

There's my husband, Greig. He's a student in his first year of dental school, a tall handsome young man. His parents were alcoholics and he was raised, I should say saved, by his grandmother. Not being worldly, he is rather impressed with my father, a charismatic businessman and real estate entrepreneur.

There's my father. William K. Maas, Sr., whose top priorities in life had proven to be business, real estate, gambling, and golf, in that order. Neither his children nor my Mother made the top four.

There's Marge, his second wife, my step-mother. She was a pretty woman, soft and sweet, having been swept up by my father's charm years before. By this time she realized she had married a man just like her ex-husband, who was also named Bill. Both Bills were successful businessmen who undervalued her. She and I shared a kindred spirit, both undervalued by my father, so we shared a bond as bona fide members of The Be-Wary-of-Bill Maas Club.

The Time Share Tour.

Dad was proud of having become a successful commercial real estate businessman, buying and selling motels. Since he had come from a poor farm in rural Iowa, he liked to show off his self-made acumen. As for this trip, I believe he wanted to impress my husband.

So Dad invited him to a timeshare tour talk in Arkansas. The invitation came to Greig rather than me, typical of Dad's pointed view that the man of the family made the decisions. It pissed me off royally, but not enough to turn down a free vacation.

Dad also wanted to check out a motel overlooking Rogers Lake as a possible acquisition. And the Ozarks area interested him because of its temperate climate, which would allow him to play golf year-round. Iowa was a lot colder in the winter.

All four of us took an eight-hour road trip together to get to Bella Vista Village. I might add that since my father was driving, I knew better, from childhood experience, than to drink anything before we left town, or in the car, because he did not like to stop once we were on the road.

I'd never been to Arkansas or the south. The strong Arkansas vernacular threw me for a loop. I'd say hi to someone. They'd ask where I "hailed from", a phrase I had never heard before. "Iowa City, Iowa," I'd say. And they'd say something like, ... Oh, Ioway..., never been there, or ... Ioway, my pap told me they grow potatoes there. It was clear they had no idea Iowa was where corn grew and was only two states away, and Idaho, where potatoes grew, was clear across the country. I didn't bother to try and correct anyone on the way to pronounce Iowa, or wrong state or potatoes thing.

The people sounded like country bumpkins to me, from some cheesy TV show. I am ashamed to say I was being an Iowa snob, feeling an advantage as a traveler getting a free vacation in a beautiful place where according to my Dad, deals were just waiting to be plucked off a tree.

Having never been to a time-share presentation, I didn't know what to expect. My husband and I agreed to go on the talk and tour. On the long drive to Arkansas, Marge and I had shared quiet conversation in the back seat while our husbands were engaged in loud talk in the front. We shared the hope that my father wouldn't embarrass us or himself at the resort. We were both familiar with his arrogance, impatience with others and short fuse.

We showed up at our appointed time for the ninety-minute timeshare pitch and were introduced to a salesman with a strong Arkansas accent. I will call him Dave-with-the-drawl. Dave didn't stand out in any special way from the other salesmen that congregated near the front desk. He was no taller than the rest, not short either, but rather innocuous. His light brown hair blended right into his pale complexion and his attire which was blandly consistent with others. There were no saleswomen in the array of beige polyester suits. Even if there had been one, and we were assigned to her, I'm certain Dad would've demanded a man.

Ushered to a round table by Dave, he offered us drinks. Then he lifted the phone to give the order to have someone bring them while he arranged his papers, handed us some brochures, and started his presentation. Dave didn't seem fully indoctrinated yet and was a little nervous in his spiel, probably fairly new at this. He laid out a beautiful array of documents, pictures, notepaper and pencils, a perfectly arranged road map. He didn't see any curves coming. Neither did I.

About twenty minutes in, Dad took over, pumping Dave with questions. Dave struggled to come up with answers to the rapid fire questions, beginning to sweat at the temples. He clearly wasn't used to going off script. Poor young Dave never made it to the point where the pressure side of his practiced sales pitch would kick in.

I witnessed the tide turn as Dad took over. It was starting to sink in that he didn't intend to buy a timeshare. I think Dave must have felt it because now Dad was leaning forward, and Dave was shrinking back. A few minutes before he'd had been talking confidently, flipping papers over, and handing Dad pictures and documents to support what he was saying.

Now, Dave just sat back in his black leather office chair, his hands gripping the ends of the chair arms as if he was bracing himself. A more experienced salesman or manager might have pegged Dad as a gift seeker by this time. That's a term in the business for people who come for the prize, which in this case was a free weekend stay. But suave, smart, and manipulative, Bill Maas would squeeze more than full value out of any offer, and I could see he wasn't really in it just for the free stay. This had become an intel mission. Even I was starting to squirm as Dad pressed on. I simultaneously loathed and admired him. I didn't like the way he was pushing Dave but respected his capability to take control while merely appearing curious. And I could also see that Dave-with-the-drawl would do just about anything to sell him a little piece of heaven at Bella Vista.

So, my maiden voyage on a timeshare tour turned out to be quite an education. I might have seen it coming if I had known a timeshare tour sales pitch is much like buying a car. I've since been to timeshare presentations and experienced the full dance. The prospective buyer is subjected to pointed questions and statements intended to flood the joy center of the brain with visions of sumptuousness in such a purchase. If still resistant, there's last-minute pressure applied. The manager is called in and the dance continues between the salesman and the manager, one playing a form of good cop and the other better cop applying all their learned skills to get you to sign the dotted line. As a woman, I was often subjected to insults like, "How can you possibly turn down such a great deal?" The implication was always clear, though unspoken - *You idiot*.... It all comes down at the end to desperate offers of incentives, a test for the potential buyer, salesperson, and manager, matching wills against stamina. If you can still resist all the pressure, well, you'll see what happens. It happened to us.

This tour became a marathon of wills. The push-pull that usually happens at the end of a tour had begun prematurely, because my father started doing the pushing.

While appearing affable, he was quite cunning, well-seasoned and ready for any objection Dave-with-the-drawl might raise.

After about an hour, the first phase of the timeshare tour was behind us and we were all ushered into a six-person golf cart to tour the development view available units. The warm breeze and ride felt good after being trapped at the crowded table in a room full of crowded tables. The cacophony of conversations had reached the din of a busy restaurant. And although I was somewhat intrigued by Dad's acumen, and Dave-with-the-drawl's persistence, the air in the room was sucked up by loud talk and testosterone.

We race-walked through six available units, not because Dave was pushy. He would have liked to continue his sales pitch. But Dad seemed to be in a hurry, showing little interest in the layouts or decor. Once back in the golf cart at the end of this whirlwind tour, , Dad turned to Dave, "There's an airstrip here, right, Dave?"

"Yes," Dave boasted, "we have a 1350-foot strip and small hangar on the North side. It can handle any small plane. Lots of our members fly in."

My father was truly interested in the airstrip, having been a World War II Navy pilot and owning a share in a private plane. Dave headed back toward the sales pavilion saying he would show us some pictures. But Dad wanted to see the airstrip.

"We can't get there in this cart;" Dave said, "we'd have to leave the development, go in a car." The discouraging tone led me to believe Dave didn't want to do that. I sensed it was probably against regulations.

But Dad insisted. He knew the small private airport

was available for use by Bella Vista owners as well as others and wanted to check it out. So once back at the center, Dave ushered us into his big sedan, he and Dad in the front seat, Marge, me and my husband in the roomy backseat.

He drove us to the hangar and airstrip. Instead of getting out to look through a fence, Dad said he wanted to see the strip closer, to drive or walk its length.

Dave said, "Can't do that, Bill. A permit is required to get to the strip side of the hangar. And we can't walk on the landing strip." But then, the ever-accommodating Dave-with-the-drawl offered to drive us out and around where we could view the airstrip from the other end and have a full view of the approach. This required going off road into a big open field that was grassy, muddy, and full of bumpy ruts, every one of which I could feel through the floor. Seatbelts were not required and we were joustled about. The three of us in the backseat shared eyerolls.

Dave parked about a football field away from the end of the runway. No one got out. We just sat there, motor running, as my father asked more questions. But then we heard a whirrrrrrr coming, and through the back window could see a small plane approaching. Dave heard it too and immediately hit the gas, doing a quick one-eighty, spun the wheels a few rounds, and brought his big low riding sedan to the edge of the field and back onto the road, shaking us up in the back seat. Seatbelts were not required back then and it was teeth jarring. As we passed over each big rut, the car seemed to grunt. By the time we got to the road, there was a constant grating that discouraged any further conversation.

Once back at the welcome center, we were hurried

up to the sales room. Dave probably expected a sale. He had gone above and beyond. But Dad had lost interest in talking purchase, and wore his impatience on his sleeve. In short order, a manager joined us and tried to follow through with a sale, but without success. It was a painful but quick dance.

So, with a pasted smile and rehearsed "It was great to meet you," the manager threw in the towel and handed us off to a clerk. A 'she', this time, without friendly banter, ushered us down some stairs and through a long, poorly lit hallway. It felt like a "walk of shame". She deposited us in what I know now, after having much more experience in time share presentations, to be an "exit room". I also know now that the others, ecstatic time-share buyers, would have been high upstairs somewhere toasting with champagne and eating donuts in a celebration room with a 360-degree view of the resort. And that they would leave the same way they came, through the elegant reception room.

The exit room was small, and tidy, a simple check out desk, no chairs, no décor, a cold room with an exterior door. Before we were to be allowed final exit, there was one more bit of business left to do. That was to get the certificate for the free weekend stay in the Bella Vista Unit. The male clerk, dressed in a polo shirt and khakis, gave it his all to try one more time to sell us something, a late, great value. We could revive the incentives and purchase within a week, or go back to Bella Vista anytime in the next year, and sit through another presentation, in exchange for a mere five hundred dollars to be paid right then.

Impatient, Dad declined, less than politely. But he

had to sign a waiver saying he relinquished all claim to the incentives, the trip back, and would be prohibited from signing up for any more timeshare tours for a year. Without this, we would not get the certificate for the free stay, and would have to pay for lodging, over one thousand dollars for the long weekend. He signed, and then the clerk in the polo shirt pointed to the back door.

It opened at the back of the sales center, directly onto poorly maintained landscaping and a narrow strip of cement along the building I wouldn't call a sidewalk. One would have to be less than a foot wide to make full use of it. We had to navigate this narrow walkway and dead plants and shrubs to get around to the front of the building and back to our car. Penance.

It was a quiet drive to a nearby restaurant where we had lunch. Not much conversation there either. On the way back to our rooms at the resort, we passed a car repair shop. I could see through the open bay door. There was Dave's blue behemoth, high on a lift. I felt for Dave, having had to face off with my nervy father at such a young age in his career. I wondered if he got in trouble for driving us out onto the field near the airstrip. I also wondered if the timeshare company insurance covered personal vehicles injured on the job. Probably not.

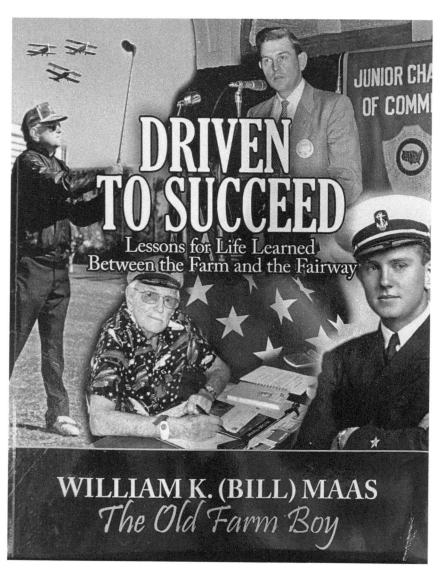

DRIVEN TO SUCCEED

Lessons for Life Learned
Between the Farm and the Fairway

JUNIOR CHA
OF COMM

WILLIAM K. (BILL) MAAS
The Old Farm Boy

Driven to Succeed – He did a good job telling his story.

DAD AND THE
$47.40 PAPERBACK

*I couldn't help myself. I knew it was wrong,
me giggling, but my frenzied brain was
sending me ridiculous messages …*

After Dad got to be a certain age, he couldn't continue to do the things that had been more important to him than what was going on in our lives, my brother and sister and I. So, he started reaching out to us, rather begging for attention. I started to call him a couple of times a month, just to check in. One time in the summer of 2017 he called me. It took me by surprise, but shouldn't have, because I'd been traveling for a few weeks and hadn't called him. It was 5:30 AM and I had to fumble around a bit to get my hands on the phone. When someone calls this early, I don't have time to stop and think maybe this is a Robo call and let it ring. My mind goes right to, "Uh Oh. Who died?" To be kind, Dad waited until it was 7:30 in Arkansas, forgetting, I assume, that it's only 5:30 in the morning in California. Without any opening courtesies he said,

"Did you get my book?"

"What book are you talking about?"

"The book I wrote about my life."

"Not yet, I didn't know you finished it."

"It is finished and you should've gotten a big yellow

envelope by now. Barbara and Will got their books a week ago."

"I don't think so, but I just got back from vacation. I haven't gone through all of my mail yet. It might be here. I'll let you know later today when I go through my mail. I'm upstairs right now and my mail is downstairs."

"It's in a big yellow envelope, why don't you go and check right now."

"I'm in bed. It's 5:30 am."

So he went on. He told me that it had been released and it was on Amazon, or so he had been told by his editor. I asked him if he had looked yet to see it. He told me no. He was pretty savvy with the Internet but mostly around email, making bets, football fantasy, and checking his investments. I don't even know if he knew how to get to Amazon.

I told him I would look, and I did, while we were on the phone. I was on my iPhone so I could search and talk at the same time. I asked him the title.

"Driven to Succeed."

I typed in "driven to succeed."

About fifty titles came up.

At the top of the list was: Driven to Succeed: How Frank Hasenfratz Grew Linamar from Guelph to Global by Rod McQueen. *Wow,* I thought, *can't even begin to pronounce that!*

So I started with the second title, rattling off a few as I scrolled. "Hmmm, there are a lot of books that come up, but I don't see yours. There's "DRIVEN TO SUCCEED: An Inspirational Memoir of Lessons Learned Through Faith, Family and Favor", by HATTIE N. WASHINGTON, "Driven: How to Succeed in Business and in Life" by Robert Herjavec, several more Driven to Succeed books, by or about famous people including Oprah and Arnold Schwarzenegger."

I kept scrolling, "There's 'Driven to Succeed: Powering Your Way to Prosperity as an Insurance Agent' by James Brown, 'Driven: My Unlikely Journey from Classroom to Cage, 'How I Made it' as a writer, athlete, singer, actor; these went on and on.

"Well, dad, I'm not seeing your book, let me try something different." So I put in "Driven to Succeed, William K. Maas" and voila! There it was!

"I found it dad!" By now, I was wide awake and even excited to see it right there, on Amazon. I could sense his chest puffing, his pride deepening, now that I saw it.

"Driven to Succeed: Lessons For Life Learned Between The Farm And The Fairway."

"Nice," I said, and then started giggling. I had seen the price.

"It says, "Paperback $47.40. Wow," I said.

It struck the absurdity meter. Just one more among so many times. I couldn't help myself. I knew it was wrong, me giggling, but my frienzied brain was sending me ridiculous messages, because it was typical for Dad to overvalue his stuff. Images flickered by and hijacked my sensitivity; like the stressful office garage sale which gave him shingles, , his trip to the famous pawn shop in Las Vegas where he didn't have a prayer of meeting the TV star owners, and his forcing my sister to take some clocks to the Antiques Roadshow when it came through Rogers only to find out they were not antiques...

Dad had no idea what was going on at my end when my giggles turned into a full blown laugh, but found it contagious. He started laughing with me. The idea that he didn't even know why he was laughing made me laugh even harder. I choked out, "Dad, this is the most expensive paperback I've ever seen on Amazon!"

I just couldn't stop now, nor could he.

"However," I continued in fits and starts, "I see it is listed with the rare and collectible, so there's that."

And we both started laughing again, the implications clear.

Then he said, in all seriousness: "Well, it covers ninety-three years. It's a great bargain."

That relit me and pretty soon he and I were both in a bona fide belly laugh.

"I get that, but still ..." I couldn't help myself, it was just rolling out of me now, "$47.40 for a paperback? That's the most expensive paperback I've ever seen! How did you come up with that price?"

"My editor said if we kept it under $50.00 that would be good, it's supposed to be some kind of psychological thing."

Still sputtering, I responded, "Oh, I can see now it is strategically priced at $47.40. If it was $49.99 that might've been a dealbreaker."

I lost it again. He followed suit while asking his caregiver to get him a Kleenex. He was laughing so hard. Me too, and I reached for one at my end. Once I calmed down, wiping my eyes with a tissue, I still couldn't talk without laughing, but soldiered on," How many do you think you will be able to sell at that price?"

"Well," he said, "I'd like to get my investment back." He had always been a businessman, in it for the profit all his life, but at this stage apparently, he would be happy to settle for return on investment. That tickled me again.

I quickly calculated in my head, if you divide the cost of making the book, which I assumed was somewhere around $5000 based on my own experience, and hoped to sell a hundred copies at $50.00 a piece, that would do it.

"How many books were published, dad?"

"One hundred."

Check! So I wondered aloud, "Dad, I don't know. Selling one hundred books at $50.00 each might be setting the bar a tad high."

Maybe I was harsh, finding something he was so invested in so funny. But I have to admit it felt good to share a belly laugh with him. That didn't happen very often.

We were calming down now, both of us.

I said, "I'll go downstairs, Dad. And check to see if there's a big yellow envelope in my mail. This is a pretty special book."

I pulled on my slippers and robe and plodded downstairs to look at my mail while he stayed on the line. He really wanted to know if I got this book.

Sure enough, it was in the stack of mail. I plucked the yellow padded envelope out of the stack and carried it upstairs. I ripped it open by the phone so he would hear me and know that I hadn't opened it before. I wanted to make sure that he didn't think I had gotten the book and just set it aside, not excited to get it.

I did know he was writing this book because on visits to Arkansas, he'd asked me to sit in on a couple of sessions with the college student who was doing the ghost writing. It took about three years to bring the project to fruition. Of course, it was a big deal for Dad to have a college student and editor gush over his life experiences. He craved that admiration from all his children, including me. But because we all felt abandoned while he lived his big life, it was not forthcoming.

Now, running my fingers over the textured satin finish of the cover, admiring the montage of photos, I said, absorbing some of his pride, "Nice cover. Looks impressive, very professional." I started leafing through the book. It was well done. Somehow, though, it flipped open right in my lap to page 72, the full document, his navy discharge form.

I scanned it as I was talking to him. And said, "Yikes, dad, did you know there is a full navy discharge form in the book, unredacted?"

"What does unredacted mean? I gave them all my notebooks full of documents and papers and pictures. It's part of the book."

"But dad, it has your navy ID number, your Social Security number, your full name, and it seems a little scary given that we live in a world where identity theft is a common thing. Nothing is blacked out. That's what redacted means, to have sensitive information blacked out."

I sensed an immediate change in the temperature of the room, except that we were not in the same room, we were two thousand miles apart. The levity was all gone. He saw this as criticism, and reacted with silence.

But I thought it pretty important so I charged ahead, "I would think your editor would've thought to blackout this personal information. They have a responsibility to their authors. It's called redacting personal information."

His old self returning, a chill melted the joy center, I could tell he was not really happy with me for pointing this out.

He responded, gruffly this time, "I'll talk to the editor. What page is it on?"

"Page 72," and I went on, because I needed to make one more point, even if it was offending him, "I would ask her to pull back all of the copies that have been distributed so far, fix that page, and any other personal information that is in there, and redistribute it. That was carelessness, and probably legally actionable. You don't have to worry about any copies you have given to friends and family, probably, but there are strangers out there who might jump on this." I figured at $50.00 a pop the risk was probably small that any had sold yet, but felt the error should be corrected by the Editor for all books sold by her company or Amazon.

Words like legally actionable, tend to slip out because of my years as a lawyer. I resisted "You could sue if she doesn't do anything," because that was too typical a go to in my profession, and not worth much here. I knew he really admired his editor and would not complain. I'm pretty sure he shrugged my comments off the minute he got off the phone. Dad had a way of filtering things. Anything he didn't want to hear just floated away.

[Note: The book was released on his birthday, March 25, 2017, and is still listed on Amazon today (April 3, 2020). He passed away December 12, 2019. The price is $21.94. The ad says there are two books available at that price. Interestingly, his book popped up as the third entry in the "Driven To Succeed" category. I guess it's true that one's fame often waits until they are gone to emerge.]

The coins ritual was one of the activities
that would help pass the time.

DAD AND THE COINS RITUAL

*If I'd try to hurry the process along by
reaching for a coin when he was busy fondling
another, I'd get a dirty look and pull my
hand back like I'd touched a hot potato.*

My father loved money. Not just money, but every-thing having to do with it. To him, big spending signified entitlement, status, wealth, and security, even at times when he didn't have the bank account to back it up. His fondness extended into his corpora, collecting antique coins, two-dollar bills, IOUs, quarters, dimes, gambling chips, and Mexican pesos. He took pleasure in making deals, gambling, and making occasional loans at a profitable interest rate to family or employees. My brother and sister and I knew that we took a backseat to my father's business and other interests.

When I was thirty, I called him to let him know I was coming back to Iowa for a visit. I told him I'd get a car at the airport and come to see him first, then go to Mom's. They lived a half hour from each other. He told me he'd just acquired a motel and a rental car company came with it. He offered to get me a car, insisting I should have the same kind of car I drove at home. "Wouldn't that be great," he'd said. And I said, "Sure, that'd be nice."

Upon my arrival in Cedar Rapids, Iowa, I took a taxi to his office. He welcomed me at the door and ushered me in to sit. We chatted a bit, catching up, and then he said, "Luckily, I was able to get a Pacer." Sliding the keys on top of some papers across the big desk toward me, he continued, "it was more expensive, but I think you'll like it." And then came the punch line, "Will you be paying by check or credit card?"

I was an adult, with two children, a job, and had managed to move across the country and re-establish myself in California, yet here it was. He could still catch me off guard. Make me a little crazy. I choked back tears thinking, *yeah, I see, just another deal.* Holding my emotions, I leaned over the contract and keys, and looked him in the eye, picked up the phone on his desk, dialed my mother's number, and said, "Mom, I am at Dad's office. Can you come and get me right away?" She lived in Iowa City, twenty-five miles away, but was there in less than a half hour. She'd dropped what she was doing and got in the car, no explanation needed. She'd been married to him for fifteen years.

Over the next thirty years, he lived his life and I was busy with mine. I visited him once or twice a year. He'd often ask me to take him places like the bank. Every so often he'd make a trip there to pick up a bag of quarters. One time I went in with him. He strolled into the small bank, and announced to the girls working the windows, "Got any good quarters in this month?" The young girls seemed charmed, all smiles and giggles. They apparently catered to him and had set aside rolls of quarters for him.

"Don't know if there's any quarters of the states you need, Bill, but we just got some new ones in," one of the girls said as she handed over some rolls in exchange for a fifty-dollar bill. Dad was on an eternal search for valuable coins and minted quarters to round out his state quarter collections. One could buy a full set of State Quarters mounted on a United States map board for about twenty bucks. But for him, there was no fun in that. He liked the hunt, the gamble.

"It's like panning for gold," he said to me. I didn't know the difference between a quarter worth $10,000 and a quarter worth twenty-five cents, and digging through quarters didn't excite me. Sometimes Dad would take me around his house and point with his cane to low antique tables that had glass cases for tops. Each was littered with watches, medallions, trinkets, bobbles, gambling chips, foreign money, and coins. He'd say, "Someday, Beth, when I'm gone, you and Will and Barbara can go on a treasure hunt for valuables in the cases. Some things are not worth much, but some are antiques. It'll be fun for you kids."

That wasn't my idea of fun.

Two-dollar bills were always special to Dad because he believed they were lucky. He gave me a two-dollar bill every time I visited him. He'd write his name and the date on the bill for even more luck. I've always kept one inside the flap on the visor of my car. I figure it can't hurt. Unfortunately, Dad passed before the initiation of the Donald Trump two-dollar bill and 45th President Coin & Currency set that came out in 2020. One can even join the club. Dad would have undoubtedly become a lifetime member.

Dad collected all kinds of coins, and at one time or another mentioned investing in gold. There was always an air of secrecy around his wealth. Even as co-trustee of he and my step-mother's trust; I never had a clear sense of his net worth. He carried mystery around rumors about gold bars with him to the grave. None ever turned up. My step-sister, Lynn, was sure he had buried some under the house. But she was known to tip more than a few so no one believed her.

Every time I visited, I stayed three days, and there were three rituals. My first day, there was always talk about his trust. He'd go over documents and papers, but focus mostly on what he wanted for a funeral service, party, and final words said about him. On the second day, I'd take an inventory of his stuff which I did with a methodical walk through his house and garage, opening doors, drawers, and closets. I'd take hundreds of pictures. By or on the third day, we'd go through his coins. The coins ritual was a relief, even though tedious. It gave me a break from his constant channel surfing between golf, football, baseball and Fox News. It was a welcome diversion. I didn't begrudge Dad his Fox News or sports time on TV. However, conversation over it always became a competition. He'd turn up the TV to catch something he didn't want to miss, right when I was in the middle of a sentence, or I'd talk loud, over the TV noise, if there was a point I wanted to make. It was exhausting.

The coins ritual had a reverence about it. Everything was turned off; everything slowed down. There couldn't be any outside noise or distraction. He'd open the door to it by saying, "Beth, maybe you can help me update my list of coins."

"Okay," I'd say, I'll go get them. Where are they?"

It was a fair question as they got moved around. There was a time when he kept them in his garage in crumpled brown paper bags. He justified that with, "If I'm robbed, a thief would think crumpled brown paper bags were trash."

I thought: *but it's dark in there, Dad. Any thief will probably trip over the bags and realize there was something in there besides trash, did j'ya think of that?*

But what I said to him was, "Dad, if there's a fire, the bags are going to burn up and leave the coins exposed. The fireman or anyone doing cleanup might steal them." I could envision a fireman's great big jacket pockets jingling with coins. Then I said, "If you want to keep them in the garage, at least put them in the metal file cabinets."

"No," he said, "That's the first place a thief would look."

Dad's logic often befuddled me, but they were his coins and he could do with them what he wanted. One time, my sister and I made the mistake of trying to help secure his collection. We met in Arkansas and spent a few days to help organize his life. We arranged for a bank box for his coins. But they never made it to the bank. As soon as we left town, Dad canceled the bank box and got a refund. He didn't see any point in paying the bank money to keep his coins. And besides, he wanted them where he could get at them, to touch and feel and see them. He just waited until we left town to make that declaration.

At least he moved them out of the garage. They made their way to his sock and underwear drawers, packed neatly in small boxes. Dad's bedroom, oddly enough, was pristine, everything in its place. No clutter.

Even though small, the boxes were heavy if you tried to carry them all at once. After dad started using a walker, I borrowed it for a transport vehicle. Otherwise, I would have had to make ten trips back and forth to the bedroom.

I'd roll the walker all the way down the long hallway into his bedroom, look where he had described boxes to be, retrieve them from the drawers, stack them neatly on the walker seat, and roll it back to the living room to within arm's reach of Dad's favorite chair. Space around him was cleared so there was room to stack boxes. He had a lap desk on his knees. I sat in a chair close by, Ipad on my lap.

The ritual unfolded methodically. Dad would open one box of coins and fan them out on his lap tray, like a blackjack dealer would fan out a deck of cards on the table. Many were in individual plastics. If there was a stack of coins, he'd carefully remove the stack from the baggie, remove the many bands securing the stack one by one, place the bands back in the baggie, and set the stack of coins on the tray. He didn't fan these coins out. It seemed he didn't want to mess up the order of the stack.

Going through one box or one stack at a time, he'd pick up a coin, examine it closely, and tell me the date and what kind of a coin it was. I would look it up on my Ipad to see what its value was. Some coins were worth face value, others more. Dad had a comprehensive hand-scribbled list. None of the values I quoted seemed like any surprise to him. He knew his coins well. Sometimes I'd try to hurry the process along reaching for a coin so I could check out the value while he was fondling another. But responding to his frown, I'd pull my hand back like I'd touched a hot potato. He wouldn't be hurried.

His collection was worth around ten thousand dollars, consistent with what his well-worn list said. If he'd sold a coin he'd mark a check beside it. But there weren't many checkmarks the last time I saw the list.

One time, after a few hours of fondling coins, he came

across a box I hadn't seen before. It looked like a flat, small, metal bank box, and it was locked. I thought maybe we'd save that for next time because we'd been at the coins ritual already for a couple hours, but Dad was curious. He really wanted to know what was in that box. I asked him if he had a key. Nope. So he had me hunt. Back through his underwear drawers I went, careful not to mess up the order, while he looked through the baggies and pouches around him. No key turned up.

He said, "I don't think I would've locked the key inside, but maybe I did."

"Maybe," I said but I was really thinking *oh boy, here we go*.

"I need something flat, or sharp," he said, "like a screwdriver. Maybe I can pick the lock or pry it open."

"Where would I find something like that?" I asked.

"Probably in the garage or maybe in one of the drawers in the kitchen."

I knew that every drawer in the kitchen was a mess and the garage was worse.

"I'll get a steak knife," I said.

Turns out Dad didn't have any steak knives. But I did find a tool that looked like a punch with a screwdriver handle on it in the junk drawer and took that into the living room.

Dad poked around at the lock. I tried too. We dubbed the box "Pandora's Box", having no idea what was inside it. The punch didn't work so I went back to the kitchen and looked around some more. I found another unidentifiable tool in the junk drawer that had a little hook on the end. I brought that to Dad. I was joking with him while he was trying like heck to get the box open. We pondered what treasures might be in that box both thinking it must be something valuable to be in a locked box.

Not one to give up, Dad finally got the box open. He lifted the lid. There was the key right on top of the pile in a little baggie stapled to a note that said "NOTICE! READ THIS!" The note also said

CAUTION
DO NOT LOCK BOX
WITH KEY
BEFORE CLOSING BOX.

I guess Dad didn't read the note.

I didn't see a gold bar or anything else in the box that looked valuable. I was about ready to end the session and chuck everything back in his underwear drawers but Dad wanted to go through the box. That led to a walk down memory lane. I'll just hit the highlights.

There were stacks of one and five-dollar chips from various casinos in Las Vegas, many of which are no longer there. In addition, I saw two black chips with $100 imprinted on them. He told how he won big by putting a dollar on his lucky number on a roulette table his first time entering a casino. And he won the hundred-dollar chips at the craps table. They were in a baggie with a scribbled note that had the date he won them, the name of the Casino, and the name of the friend he was with at the time, Jimmy Williams. Jimmy was perhaps his closest friend, and had passed away. Tears formed at the corners of his eyes as he took the chips out of the baggie and rolled them around in his hand. While he was reminiscing, I thought back too. There had been times he heard me mention I was going to Las Vegas for a business trip. He would give me a two-dollar bill to put on number thirty-two on the roulette table. He'd say, "But you have to split the pot with me." I couldn't tell if he was joking. But I never won so it didn't matter.

Also in the box were some men and women's diamond rings with written appraisals. Nothing of great value. These he had won in poker games.

The last item he pulled out was a crumpled sandwich size baggie with a scribbled hand-written note in it. He handed the baggie to me and I turned it over to see what looked like a dirty ten-dollar bill with heavy tread shoe prints on it. I was puzzled; not sure what kind of reaction was expected. Dad reached out and took it back, pulled the note out, and read, "Walmart Parking Lot, Rogers, Ark. July 11, 2010."

"I couldn't believe it," he said, "I sat there in my car and watched five people step on this ten-dollar bill and no one bent over to pick it up. Ten Dollars!"

Even I could feel the folly in that.

Then, suddenly, he was tired. I stacked the boxes back onto the walker and started down the hall toward his bedroom. "Be sure and put them back in the right drawers," I heard. It sounded like he was drifting off. I returned them to what I thought were exactly the right drawers placing them underneath neatly folded piles of boxer shorts and socks.

Within his last few years, Dad tried to send his coin collection home with me more than once, for "safe keeping". He wouldn't accept a bank box in Rogers and I figured if they were stolen from his bedroom, so be it. He had lots of caregivers in and out. But I knew him. It was not a good idea to take responsibility for his coins. So I declined. I didn't want to be the last one to have his coins. Lynn, my step-sister, was hungrily awaiting her inheritance and capable of spinning tales and making waves.

Most importantly, I suspected that Dad would want the collection back in Arkansas as soon as I got home to California with it. My sister fell for it though. One time when she and her husband were visiting, Dad sent his coin collection home with her to Santa Fe. She thought he wanted help selling the collection, and secured an appraisal for him. She sent the info to Dad. He complained that he'd already had them appraised, and it was for more money, and he wanted the coins back immediately. He acted like she had some nefarious intent. She was so angry that she and her husband got in their car and drove twelve hours to Arkansas to take the coins back to Dad. They dropped them off at his house and turned around and drove back home to New Mexico without staying over.

That was the end of that. I don't know where the coins ended up. They weren't in his drawers when he passed away. Mysterious, rather like the gold bars.

Hoarder or collector, the question kept coming up.

DAD - HOARDER
OR COLLECTOR?

One time he saw me grab a mug from the railing in the living room to use for coffee. Man, it was dusty! As I blew the dust off and sneezed, he said in an accusatory tone. "There are cups in the kitchen for coffee."

When I visited Dad in 2018, I looked around his large living room and noticed out loud that it seemed he had a lot of new plants. What had caught my eye were many fake plants in the sunroom that at one time had been green, I was pretty sure. They suffered a bluish tinge. And it seemed like they had multiplied since the last time I was there. He said he had become more of a plant lover so he added a few plants. But he followed a bit defensively with, "… well really, I just moved some things around."

Lots of our conversations revolve around his things. He was tired of hearing from my brother and sister and me that he had too many things. So yes, he had a right to get a little defensive. We'd said way too much about it, made sarcastic comments, and made fun of some of his "treasures", and yes, we probably had stepped over a line.

Dad was the master collector in our family. He had said more than once he hoped we would turn his house into a museum when he went, but usually added a little spitefully, "but I know you won't do that." He fretted way too much about what would happen to his possessions when he died.

Sometimes "things" became a battleground. For example, Dad was a big Donald Trump fan, in fact, I fancied him a "Trump mini-me". My brother Will was a Trump-hater. Dad knew he could always get under Will's skin just by mentioning Trump. He seemed to take pleasure poking at Will, like the time he gifted him the book, "Donald Trump, Think Like a Champion," and added his personal inscription. The book ended up in the stacks of books and memorabilia on Dad's big round table in the middle of the room for years after, a constant reminder of my brother's rejection of the gift.

I went the opposite way. Knowing Dad worshipped Trump, on one Father's Day I gave him a Trump bobble-head doll. I thought it quite a joke. But the doll was given a place of honor on the banister by Dad's favorite chair, along with other favored President bobbleheads. He had quite a collection. Nixon, Clinton, Reagan, Bush, both George and George W. and now Donald Trump. With Fox News on twenty-four-seven and the Donald right there in the lineup of favorites, Dad was among his people. But one time I went to visit, and noticed the Trump bobble-head was missing from the lineup.

"Where'd Donald go?"

"He's over there, standing in the corner by the fireplace."

I looked over and he was indeed standing with his back to us, face to the corner.

"What's Trump doing over there?"

"He cheated on his wife."

Apparently, Dad had a moment of moral introspection causing him to draw the line for Trump. I guess he forgot that when my siblings and I were in our teens, he left our mother for a younger woman.

Many times before and during visits, he mentioned he would like to get rid of some of his things, pass them on. Talking about his stuff became a thing. He called similar items like clocks, teaspoons, golf balls, trinkets, bobble-heads, etc., his "collections". I called them stuff.

I don't believe he discussed his stuff much with my brother or sister, but talks about his trust, his posses-sions and preservation and distribution of his things were common topics of conversation between us. Probably be-cause I was co-trustee of his family trust. These chats were welcome, providing a good diversion when, as was common, he would begin to criticize someone in the fam-ily. He was perturbed that neither of my siblings appreci-ated the value of collections. Maybe he talked about me the same way to them. The truth was I found exploring his emotional baggage around possessions much more interesting than the stuff itself. In fact, I was working on a collection of essays called, "The Stuff About Stuff."

Besides, I was somewhat of a collector too, happy to contribute to his stash by sending him about thirty mugs I had gathered on my travels. This was only half my own collection of about sixty. I would've sent him all of them but that seemed pretty self-serving after being critical about him having so much unnecessary stuff around. But he had opened up the door to it. When I asked him if he might like some more mugs, he'd said, "Yes, I would." But there were limits. The railing separating his living room from his dining room was full already. When the new treasures came he had shelves installed high on the walls in his laundry room to display the mugs I sent him. And a few other things too, of course.

One time he saw me grab a mug from the railing in the living room to use for coffee. Man, it was dusty! As I blew the dust off and sneezed, he said in an accusatory tone, "There are cups in the kitchen for coffee."

Sorrreeeeee, I thought. All he had in his kitchen cupboard for coffee were dainty china cups. After that, when I wanted a good-sized mug, I just took one off of one of the shelves in the laundry room and used it and then put it back when I was done. At Dad's house, you had darn sure better put everything back where you got it or you'd be in big trouble.

Yes, there are many stories about stuff. On the first day this trip, after mentioning the many blue fake plants, I looked around some more and spotted a faded Christmas centerpiece with tapers that had folded over into an arch. It looked like at some point it had sat in the sun too long, like the other blue fake plants. But it might have been the heat in the house, which was high. It now sat on a little table about two feet from his favorite recliner, and so in a place of some prestige. He could look at it every day. People who came in the front door could see it at first glance too. At one time, I am sure it was beautiful with red shiny balls, green plastic holly sprigs, and two white taper candles standing like soldiers at the ready. But the sprigs had faded to gray, the balls had lost their shine, and the soldiers had given up the fight. I picked it up and eyed it closely. *What could he possibly see in this tired old centerpiece?*

Lifting it toward him, I said. "Maybe this could go,

Dad. There's a difference between collecting and hoarding. What do you think? It looks like it's well past its prime. Didn't these candles used to stand up?" I ran my finger along the arch created by the apparent melting that had occurred – the tops of the tall tapers, now a bit dirty crème colored with age, had nestled back into the arrangement.

"I got that from the Country Club. They gave it to me a couple years ago after a Christmas party."

"But dad, it's long dead, the candles are done. They've collapsed. Why do you want to keep it?"

"I like it," he said. "No one else has one like it. "

"I don't doubt that," I said, a tad bit sarcastically.

But once he told me the Club gave it to him, I understood. The Club to him represented a great source of status. To the rest of us in the family, it represented an overpriced restaurant and bar, for the likes of the rich people of the Walmart family for whom this golf course community was developed. They represented to us people who have too much wealth and don't know what to do with it. The Pinnacles Golf and Country Club development he lived in was filled with monolithic homes and pseudo-castles that don't seem to be full time residences to many. Second gargantuan homes. Third, maybe? I hardly ever saw anyone around, except for a few foursomes now and then on the golf course, unless it was tournament time. During the one big Women's Professional Open Tournament each year all driveways and streets are filled with cars of guests in town for the tourneys. But that's not the norm.

For Dad, belonging to "The Club" was his idea of the epitome of success. Coming from a poor small-town Iowa farm to the big time Country Club and owning a house in a development claiming to have a Championship golf course, no less, was a dream come true. So, anything he had in his house that came from The Club was sacred.

I sat the sad looking Christmas centerpiece back on the little table, thinking maybe we would defer any more talk about the difference between hoarding and collecting to a later time.

In the course of the three days I was there, which is my sacrificial limit of tolerance with any modicum of grace, we went through the usual rituals, discussion of his business and his Trust, going through his coins, sometimes watching funny Carol Burnett/Tim Conway DVDs or pulling out his Karaoke machine.

I came home from that visit and started to write the story in the kindest terms I could about the difference between hoarders and collectors, thinking Dad was sliding down a slippery slope toward hoarder. This coincided with an article I was writing for my law newsletter about the difficulties of dealing with hoarder situations in homeowner associations. I did some research and came to the conclusion he was safe for awhile. And luckily, he didn't get out much anymore so it would be difficult to add to his museum, or dare I slip and say, mausoleum. He definitely is a collector. But a hoarder? According to the international OCD foundation, compulsive hoarding includes **all** three of the following:

A person collects and keeps a lot of items, even things that appear useless or of little value to most people, which clutter the living spaces and keep the person from using their rooms as they were intended, and cause distress or problems in day-to-day activities.

Whew I thought, he was not there yet. He loved his stuff. The house was definitely cluttered, most wall space was filled with paintings, collections, picture collages and montages, clocks on shelves, goofy signs, and trinkets. For example, one board hanging on a wall contained state souvenir spoon collections bought on road trips when we were kids. We never passed a famous blue Stuckey's tourist trap without stopping for Stuckey's ice cream and pralines, a Kachina Indian doll, and a souvenir spoon. In his house there were shelves and racks lined with mugs, golf balls, shot glasses, and on a table in the laundry room there was a five-gallon water jug filled with matchbooks from all over. It was hard to find light switches in the dark because of all the things hanging near the switches. But there wasn't really a problem moving around in the house. No stacks blocking walkways or anything like that.

Oddly enough, his bedroom was clean and stark, not an ounce of clutter. All three bedrooms were devoid of clutter, but the living spaces were a different story.

None of his clutter caused him any stress. I don't think his visitors ever said word one about it. And I quit saying much about getting rid of stuff after one of his visits to California, the best, most pleasing ever. I took him shopping for his birthday to an antique store, a pretty junky one. We spent at least two hours in this store while he admired and fondled bells, canes, clocks, snuffboxes, and trinkets, many of which he collected. He didn't complain at all, ask to sit down, or want to leave, excited like a kid in a candy shop. I became invisible. It felt like he was among friends.

We, his adult children, dreaded the day he would die leaving a houseful of stuff

PART 2

DAD BECOMES
GREAT GRANDPA

The Usual Suspects

How did Dad become Great Grandpa?
I had kids. And they had kids.

Having written a few "Dad" stories, I found that poking fun at his absurd and childish behavior was kind of fun. And I felt compelled to write about him. Writers cannot always explain what motivates them. There were other people in my life that I loved more, like my mother. But with Dad, it was a need. Even as an adult with my own family, there were still moments when I wanted to slap, scream, shush, or club him, or hurt or cry, so I wrote instead.

At the five-year reunions, Dad was surrounded by adults and children and activity, but still needed to be the center of attention. He really wanted to be in charge but there was little hope of that. When chaos reigned among the guests, he continually tried to mold the activities to fit his plans, a determined geriatric trying to herd twenty cats.

"All the world is a stage," said William Shakespeare.

While Dad struggled to control, I both observed and managed him. Dry wit, sarcasm, and humor became my tools of choice. Had anyone been aware of my directorial role it might have been obvious that I was often simply cultivating the fodder. Little did I know at the time that personal growth in an important familial relationship was actually happening. I was finding my father to be comical, in a preposterous way. I relished the new chronicles.

In recounting these stories I briefly considered fictionalizing the events, but couldn't manufacture more authentic drama and absurdity than what occurred naturally in every trip to Arkansas. I felt like the creator of a multi-act play, calling everyone together, and watching events unfold as the actors arrived, allowing for plenty of spontaneity and ad-libbing. I was not only the director, but a key performer as well, circulating among the others, scouting for juicy delicious tidbits. There was no longer any point in going head-to-head with him. In addition to comedy and drama, there was mystery. No one else knew of my secret multi-faceted role as director, co-host, instigator, prodder, parent, and child. And after each long weekend I memorialized the events. I did not want to be the only witness to the remarkable play.

It's true, I did capitalize on his childlike fits. I kept my stories close to the vest, didn't share them with him. I wasn't in it to inflict pain. I knew he wouldn't be able to laugh at his own foibles. Even in my visits between the five-year birthdays, there were always thespians for series. Great Grandpa, me, caregivers, and whoever else showed up.

I went from dreading visits to anticipating the provender to come. Emotions trivialized by him over the years became my strengths. Writing enabled me to laugh, cry, and cleanse with purpose. I learned to push back knowing that he'd bristle, throw a fit like a mad King or an impetuous child, or try to manipulate me. I was well prepared with maturity and a pen.

As time went on, I found additional ways to neutralize the effects of his robotic impractical demands. For example, he'd often come up with some scheme to tap into my legal capabilities. He was always looking for free legal advice, asking me to draft agreements for this or that, usually something ethically questionable. He was limited by a Family Trust Document that had locked up the assets he and my stepmother Marge had accumulated. When either died, the other would be entitled to continue to use the assets for living expenses for the lifestyle to which he or she was accustomed. For Dad, always pushing the envelope, the lifestyle to which he had become accustomed included golf, business and gambling. But he had to some degree contain frivolous waste of assets as he got older because of a concern of running out of money before he died. He planned to live to be a hundred years old.

He always had a list of things ready that he wanted to discuss with me when I came on visits alone. Death, Trust, business. First of all he always wanted to refine the glowing statement that would be read at a big party honoring him when he passed. Then he wanted to go over the obituary making sure to note all his accomplishments again. Those were just appetizers. Then came the main course. He always had devised some scheme to prevent his stepdaughter from inheriting anything. I understood his resistance, given that she had taken advantage of her mother's weakness when Marge was dying of ALS and managed to finagle thousands of dollars from her, accounts in Marge's name but also assets in the trust. Because the remaining assets were affected by the lock date of the trust, Dad was prevented from cutting any heirs out. So he devised scheme after scheme to move assets out of the trust. One was that he'd "sell" my siblings and I all his assets for below market value and we'd lease them all back to him for a low monthly amount, like fifty dollars. His logic was that we'd get the benefit of his assets for a low cost, and he'd get to enjoy them until he was gone. The thing was, none of us were interested in any of his assets. "Just draft me an agreement," he'd say.

I was unwilling to even consider such a thing so for years I'd just say "No." That always set him off. He'd get flippant, angry, and say something insulting like, "You're just weak. I'll ask your brother or sister to do it." Knowing neither would I'd just as flippantly respond, "Go ahead. Good luck with that." And to punish him, clear my head, and avoid more insults, I'd leave, go out for a walk, even if it was raining. It became part of "the rituals" of each visit.

However, as he got older, and I realized the visits went a lot more pleasantly if I just stopped arguing with his crazy notions. I adopted a new tactic. I'd just say "yes" to everything. . In answer to his inane requests, I'd say, "Yes Dad, sure ... how about if we do this later .... I need to get unpacked first." Or "I need to make a quick call first." Or "I need to get a cup of coffee and relax first." Or "Let's do the coins first." And then I'd do my best to fill the next three or four days with less controversial topics. "Yes ... sure Dad, ... later, ..." became a habit.

Between aging and the benefit of my buffer squad of family, the reunions evolved into a catalyst for change, helping me by giving me more stories to write, and the ability to view him through the lens of my children and grandchildren who didn't carry my years of antipathy and heavy emotional baggage. After Dad became Great Grandpa, though he was still capable of poor behavior, it was not as vexing anymore. In fact, seeing him as a new character in the play helped me unpack my baggage.

Expectations ran high for a trip to the
lake. What can possibly go wrong?

GREAT GRANDPA AND THE LAKE TOUR

As had happened before, I became the rope in a tug of war. I could see that the young were done touring and ready to eat, but Great Grandpa was not budging. I could tell by the way he set his jaw. His lunch plan was blown. It would take some finesse to get him out of the car.

Great Grandpa invited everyone to come to Arkansas for a big birthday celebration on every fifth-year birthday. He always enlisted me to help him pull this together and so it was my family that always came. On this weekend, my kids and grandkids; my sister, Barbara, and her husband Mark; and my ex-husband Greig and his family all showed up, the usual suspects. Five of the seven children were great grandchildren, and there were two others, Greig's grandchildren by daughter, Megan. Everyone was considered family.

And early this morning, all of us gathered around him. We were having coffee and eating donuts, which were Great Grandpa's breakfast of "champions". He insisted every morning that someone make the trip to Krispy Kreme and get two dozen donuts, so someone always did. We weren't really donut-for-breakfast people but neither Kristin's husband Keo nor Ryan ever needed to be asked twice. And everyone knew that if we did not eat them Great Grandpa would be eating donuts for every meal for the rest of the week, or they'd turn up next visit after sitting in the freezer a year. He was a depression survivor, he would never toss food out, especially donuts.

He had always provided us with an itinerary of plans in advance of every weekend trip. On this Saturday, a Lake Tour was on the list. To entice, he read from the tour book describing *Beaver Lake* in Rogers. "Crystal clear lake perfect for water sports and fishing nestled in the heart of the *Ozark Mountains* of Northwest Arkansas." We'd been on the Lake before, usually on a pontoon boat or having a picnic on the banks, so it sounded like fun.

As we ate and gabbed, Great Grandpa then commandeered everyone's attention by, with dramatic flair, opening up a large map of Rogers in his lap, and steadying his pen, he started pointing out the sites we would see. There was a four plex overlooking the lake he had bought and lived in for a few years with Great Grandma Marge. There was the Beaver Lake Motel, which he had owned for many years. He was adding some other drive-bys of homes of friends on the lake, a duplex he had built and was renting out, and other houses he had sold when he was a realtor. Not the kind of thing of much interest to anyone but him. He capped it off with a plan to visit a tourist attraction, War Eagle Mill. Then we would come back to town and eat at Mimi's Café, his favorite restaurant. He tapped the pen on the map as if that was final!

By this time patience in the youngsters was waning. They were antsy from all the donut sugar and torturous tour description. The parents realized that they needed to get the kids moving. And I knew I needed to get Great Grandpa moving because he was lingering with his donuts and coffee, still strolling down memory lane. He wasn't about to be moved before he was ready. That was a trait of Grandpa. He was stubborn. As soon as he realized things were not going his way, he would dig in his heels. But the families were working their way through a mountain of flip flops and heading for the front door, getting ready to go out to the vans.

When I rolled my eyes at her, my daughter Kristin looked at Great Grandpa and said, "Grandpa, we need to get the kids moving. We're going to go ahead and drive around the Lake and go on to the Mill."

This was definitely not in keeping with the "plan" laid out by Great Grandpa. He had envisioned a parade of vehicles, him in the lead car, on a grand tour taking all morning. He even had handed out walkie talkies so he could play tour guide. But that idea went out the door with the three young families who disappeared through the opening to pile into their vans in the front circular driveway. They were revving up their engines to leave in their own caravan, anxious to get on their way.

Great Grandpa was miffed that anyone had the nerve to leave the house before him. He had anticipated everyone would patiently wait while I brought his car around from the garage, and line up behind us as the lead vehicle. And so it began. I could see that once again, this was not going the way he intended, and braced myself, bit my tongue and brought the car around to the front door.

At that, he accepted that we needed to get moving, and he, his lady friend Esther, and Barbara and Mark piled into his car. Grandpa Greig and Marcia pulled up behind us, respectful of the intended "Plan". All the vans were out of sight.

Great Grandpa insisted that we still take his tour around the lake. I protested. "Dad, everyone else will get to the Mill way before we do.

But he was adamant that we do the tour of the lake. I was driving so I sped out of the driveway, Greig right behind me. It turned out to be a racing tour around the lake, Great Grandpa barking directions, pointing, and running landmarks and backstories together into the walkie talkie as fast as he could push intelligible words out. Greig and Marcia were the only audience left, besides the passengers in our car, Barbara, Mark and Esther. We got to the mill around 11:30. By that time the young families were all "milled" out having been inside the Mill, the Museum, taken the Mill hike to the river, and having taken pictures of the kids climbing on all the outside attractions. The young families were hungry and wanted to eat in the Mill café.

This put another wrinkle in Great Grandpa's grand plan to end up at Mimis for lunch. Everyone else was ready to eat at the Mill. It was okay by me. I hated Mimi's. It was always an ice box on a hot day. They cranked the AC so low that it was frigid. And I knew that no one was dressed for it. Shorts and tank tops wouldn't cut it. I had flashed back on prior visits to Mimis when Great Grandpa brought it up as part of the tour, but knew better than to mess with his grand plan. He did not like to be challenged and could be a real bear.

So the choice was to have lunch there or move on quickly to get to Mimi's before the young ones got any more restless. But Great Grandpa dug in again, "I want to tour the mill, I'm not ready to eat yet." He turned to me," And besides, there are stairs to the café and I don't want to climb stairs to eat."

As had happened before, I became the rope in a tug of war. I could see that the young were done touring and ready to eat, and that Great Grandpa was not budging. I could tell by the way he set his jaw. His lunch plan was blown. It would take some finesse to get him out of the car.

First, I tried kindness. "Dad, I think the choice left is to eat here with everyone or just let them eat here and take you back to get lunch at Mimi's. I'm hungry too."

He held firm, "But I want to tour the Mill."

The older adults, Greig, Marcia, Barbara and Mark, and Esther, hung back to see what would happen. The young families headed up the stairs, oblivious to the drama.

Then I said, a little less kind, about touring the Mill, "Not going to happen Dad if you want to eat with the group. We have to go NOW."

"Go ahead and eat," he said, pouting like a child. "I'll just sit in the car."

Feeling very unsympathetic, trying one more tactic, I told everyone else to go ahead up to the café, to save us a spot, that I'd get Grandpa up there. I could see that he was h'angry, somewhere between hungry and angry. And I didn't want to be around him either, so I gave him a simple choice.

"You can sit in the car, or tour the mill, or do whatever you want. I'll bring you a sandwich when I come back down. Or, you can come with me to the café." I turned toward the building and started to walk away.

He opened the car door and got out with a scowl. I waited for him to make sure he navigated the steps safely.

We all had lunch together upstairs at the Mill Café which was a delightful spot. We sat at long gaily decorated picnic tables with colorful fresh cut flowers and the whole place smelled of fresh baking bread and honey. And it was not freezing cold. Three cheers! Once everyone got food in them, things calmed down.

But still, it was a long, silent ride in our car back to Great Grandpa's house.

The infamous office / garage / trinket sale.
What can possibly go wrong?

GREAT GRANDPA AND GARAGE SALE SHINGLES

*At least I didn't tell him what I was thinking,
which was that I could imagine why the
lady he hired quit, that his stuff was mostly
crap, and that I figured he would eventually
have to pay someone to haul it away.*

Great Grandpa was an enigma. He caused my siblings and me much consternation. If I was allowed only three words to describe him, I would choose narcissistic, vexing, and resilient. These traits helped him to live well in his own world, but led to a plethora of trials for those around him.

In 2011, at eighty-two, Great Grandpa decided to give up his office. He had been in real estate for many years and for most of that time had a booming business buying and selling motels. However, like many, his business lost wind in the 2008 downturn, and I'm not sure it fully recovered. Driving had become iffy for him and he was getting tired. When my step-mother Marge got ALS and had to give up her townhouse with stairs, he built a duplex so she could live in half of it and he could rent out the other half. The business-investment headspace would never fully clear until he was too old to care. So he bought a couple more small duplexes in Rogers and managed those himself, with the help of his aging secretary.

Running a business gave Great Grandpa purpose.

A few years before the decision to close his office, he'd given up a large, attached warehouse where he stored "collectibles" including two classic cars: a white 1967 Cadillac Deville convertible and a third generation black Lincoln Continental. Other items included miscellaneous furniture, furnishings, and boxes stacked high, maybe a hundred or more. I don't think he knew what was in them when he sold the warehouse. I had never ventured near the stacks of furniture or boxes for fear of them toppling over and burying me. When he gave up the warehouse, he sent everything off to be auctioned. I'm quite certain he did not open the boxes before sending them off to be sold. They had been moved from place to place for God-knows-how-many years. It would've taken a lot of energy to find out what was in the boxes.

Great Grandpa still an entrepreneur at heart, finally realized he didn't really need the expense of an office anymore. All that was left to do was collect rents and arrange repairs if there was a need. June, his secretary, told him she'd be fine coming to the house and continue as his secretary. Great Grandpa really wanted me to get involved with the "business" of managing his duplexes. I was having considerable success as a landlord of two properties. I sat in once with them in the office to see what was needed. June diligently took notes on a piece of paper as Great Grandpa dictated orders. But she already had her own notes on the page so the additions had to be squeezed into the empty spaces. Her pencil notes ran around in circles and off the page. The scribbling was possibly indecipherable to the scrivener and useless to an onlooker. But she had been doing this for such a long time she could read Great Grandpa's mind even if he did not make anything clear. She'd been with him for over forty years and was probably over seventy-five herself so it wasn't easy for her either.

Letting the office go was hard on Great Grandpa but not on June. The old office equipment was all but useless. There was no chance of me moving to Arkansas and joining the business either. No reason for Great Grandpa to be driving across town either. Traffic was getting worse, and so was his driving. He was a danger to himself and others on the road.

He moved some of his office furniture to his home, his big desk and office chair, and one smaller desk, June's I think. He moved the fax machine too. And some file cabinets which went into his garage. Setting up a home office required space, and the sacrifice of his pool table. This was a tough choice for him, but his game was slipping anyway. Consistent with Great Grandpa's inability to let things go, he had the pool table moved out of his dining room twenty feet away into an open area next to his living room. This area was already full of other stuff, his player piano, bookshelves, and long brown folding tables laden with binders, books in stacks underneath.

Great Grandpa's work was pretty much all he had left. He had loved golf but his golfing days were behind him, his game spent. He loved gambling but his gambling days were on the wane. One thoughtful fellow poker player had suggested that he didn't seem to be as sharp as he used to and it might be best if he opted out of the high stakes games. Uncharacteristically, Great Grandpa listened, and took the advice. Assistance that he needed on a regular basis with medications, physical and mental therapies, getting to doctor's appointments, and diet and nutrition needs were starting to cost him quite a bit of money.

One other thing happened that had never occurred before. There was an office breakin. Not much if anything was taken. There was not much of value. No modern electronics, no money. The robbers must have left empty handed, disappointed.

So, many things led to his decision to give up the office. It had become just another place where he stored stuff: outdated office equipment, golf trophies, business-related awards dating back to his thirties when he owned a grain and feed business and also from his commercial real estate business connections.

So he decided to have a "going out of business sale". It was a glorified garage sale where items would be displayed on tables outside the office in the parking lot. He was sure this would pay off, fatten dwindling coffers. He also assumed friends and family would step up to do the work for him. However, he couldn't even garner luke-warm interest, leaving him baffled. He had no idea of the amount of work needed to prepare for and hold a garage sale. His sights were high because in his lifetime he had always willed his way to success. He was a hard worker, equipped for gambling, cavorting, negotiating real estate deals, and being the boss, but unfortunately, not for selling his stuff. Like many of us, he overvalued his possessions and office equipment, not considering it was really old, though not antique quality.

He tried to recruit helpers calling on some of his "minions" to do the work. He telephoned each of us, me and my siblings, all of whom live at least a thousand miles away, wanting us to drop everything immediately and come to Arkansas to do the work and conduct the sale. Us "minions" were not foolish enough to fly to Arkansas and muddle through this with him. We were well aware of his personality and expectations and had a hard enough time getting along with him when we were just visiting. We all urged him to pay someone to help or just donate the stuff to Goodwill and take the tax writeoff. We all offered to contribute to hiring someone, and we all also suggested considering auction as a means of selling the bulk of his stuff.

I knew from trying to assist Great Grandpa with his business in the past that the office equipment was stone age, barely operable by June, who was at least familiar with its quirks. It was not worth beans. I didn't want to be the one to tell him that a sale would be a lot of work with little return. He was not disposed to listen anyway.

Great Grandpa did find a woman who had some experience with garage sales through an ad in a local paper. I asked him what her name was. He called her "the Mexican lady". I doubt he even asked her name. She would price all of the items and be there the day of the sale to help him, for a share of the proceeds. He didn't have to pay her any money if he didn't make any money. It seemed like a good deal to him, and to me.

However, a couple days after I talked to him, he called and said "The Mexican lady quit." He said she was difficult to work with. It could have easily been the other way around. It seemed more likely to me that he either insulted or fired her, probably for underpricing his stuff. I'd seen that coming.

He did say she wanted to put a quarter on everything. I said, "Dad, people who come to garage sales don't want to spend more than a quarter or a few dollars, unless it's exceptional stuff. I've had much experience with this."

At least I didn't tell him what I was thinking, which was that I could imagine why the lady he hired quit, that his stuff was mostly crap, and that I figured he would eventually have to pay someone to haul it away. I kept my thoughts to myself, knowing that if I questioned what really happened with "the Mexican lady", he might embellish the story and claim the woman was stealing from him even though there wasn't much worth stealing. And then I would want to challenge him on his own behavior. I wasn't surprised the last chance for help had unraveled. Great Grandpa was not respectful nor appreciative of women. Especially ones he called "foreigners", those who didn't look or talk like him.

I had learned no one could win an argument with Great Grandpa, so why try. If challenged, he just lashed out or retreated to infantile behavior, or even worse, took his passive aggressive stance with, "I don't understand your problem. I'm just an easy-going guy." That declaration, which I heard more than once, would drive me bonkers.

In spite of this hiccup with help, he soldiered on and decided to do it all himself, but not without a lot of grumbling. He tried hard to play the guilt card on me and my siblings. But it didn't work.

We all stuck to our guns, advising him to donate all the stuff and take a tax credit or pay someone to haul it away. We all had experience with garage sales, knew how much work they were, and what to expect for a return. But he crowed he would make good money from this sale, and claimed we were the problem because we weren't willing to drop everything and jump on an airplane.

The day of the sale was brutal. It was hot, sticky, stressful and unproductive, according to his account of it. An email came to my siblings and me a few days after the sale took place. . Given that it was written and sent at 5 am, I am thinking he didn't get much sleep the night before.

Received 11/11/2011 at **4:59:08 A.M.** Pacific Standard Time.

"Subj: RE: howseverything going?

Hi Will, Beth and Barbara: I've just gone through the worst ten days I can remember and as a result I have a bad case of the Shingles. I had to throw away 30 years of things I really worked hard for and saved to sell when I got old so I wouldn't have to ask for financial help. If I had it to do over again I would save nothing but Gold and Silver. I always envisioned having a place to display and sell small collections but it just didn't work out that way. I had no help show up to help with the Garage sale before, during, or after the Sale even though I had given some items away to people before the sale. I received about $250.00 for all the time I put in and got a Bad case of the Shingles out of it. I still have a thousand dollars worth of stuff to give the Salvation Army next Tuesday. I spent $100.00 for medication for the Shingles and ten days of misery for all of my 30 Years of work boxing and carrying all that stuff with me all those Years. Life at the moment is a touch of "HELL ON EARTH" rather than the Bowl of cherries. I had to "Cut wood and carry water" as they say. … but … I will never, never, never give up!! Until I am put to sleep forever.

Well, have a Good Day now.
Dad"

My siblings and I all got Shingles vaccine shots.

WELCOME

Fresh-ground Wagyu beef burgers. 35+ Day aged steaks. Slow-smoked BBQ. Authentic Italian wood-fired pizzas.
We are a gourmet-casual watering hole featuring fresh, high-quality ingredients throughout our entire menu. Bring the family & give us a try today!

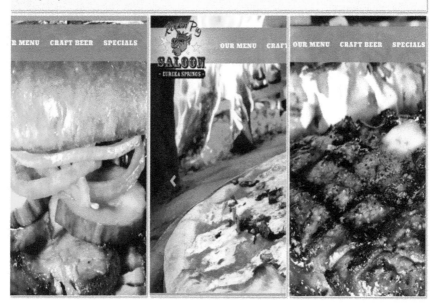

Waygu burgers, beer, and outdoor patio.
What can possibly go wrong?

GREAT GRANDPA AND THE ROCKIN' PIG

*Once we had a plan, the kids got antsy and fidgeted
by the front door impatiently wanting to leave.
Their parents went into "go mode" making sure
they each got the right flip flops out of the pile and
went to the bathroom, Great Grandpa dawdled*

On this visit to Arkansas, one of the five-year Great Grandpa birthday "extravaganzas," we planned a trip to Eureka Springs, all twenty of us. This included the usual suspects, my family (my son and daughter and their kids), Greig's family (my former husband, and his second wife, their daughter and her family), and Aunt Barbara and Uncle Mark. Eureka Springs is a fun town to visit about twenty-five miles east of Rogers as the crow flies.

The town offers an interesting mix of locals and tourists, outdoor cafes, and a well preserved historic main street. It is a popular attraction. Having been there before, I could see us strolling past the historic hotel, reaching for large bubbles released freely from a machine in front of the magic shop, sitting on benches listening to the street musicians gaily offering Bluegrass, folk, and washboard tunes for the pleasure of passers-by.

Great Grandpa wanted to take us to lunch, all twenty of us. In fact, he *insisted*. "Esther is coming with us. We'll go to Mimi's," he said, like a General issuing orders to the troops.

There was break in the ranks almost immediately. Keo, my son-in-law, got out his smartphone and brought up Yelp, a sight that provides reviews for businesses, restaurants, and the like. This was his M.O., checking reviews, looking for eateries with good food and high marks.

He found the Rockin' Pig, known for fresh-ground "Wagyu" burgers. Waygu is the proper spelling, Japanese for beef. But this was Arkansas, and The Rockin' Pig called it "Wagyu beef", ... "Prized for its marbling texture and high content of good fats like Omega-3." The ad said it's the most tender beef you can find anywhere. Also on the menu were 28 Day aged steaks, slow-smoked BBQ, authentic Italian wood-fired pizzas, and Craft Beer on Tap, Apple Blossom, Bike Rack, Fat Tire, Sierra Nevada & many more. To top off the perfection, there was a large outdoor patio.

"The restaurant received four and a half out of five stars," Keo said.

"Sounds good," a couple of us chorused. "Let's go."

"What about Mimi's?" Great Grandpa said. I knew about his love affair with Mimi's and I could tell it frosted him that his "suggestion" for the lunch outing was ignored. Mimi's Café was close to his house and I'd eaten there before with him and Esther. The food is good enough but the tables are close to each other. It's noisy and crowded and frigid. One time when we ate there it was so cold I went back to the house to get sweaters for Esther and me. I figured Great Grandpa must've been in "man-o-pause" because he was fine, and critical too. "It's not that cold," he'd said. Esther and I looked at each other and bunched up our sweaters around our necks.

I also knew that Great Grandpa did not like outdoor dining. Once Esther and I had talked him into sitting at an outdoor table at Mimi's. He tried to resist but I said, "It's two to one Dad." He gave in, but punished us by complaining the whole time about the food and picking on the waitress. I was relieved we weren't going to Mimi's.

None of us Californians wanted to be cooped up inside. It was a beautiful day. Everyone other than Great Grandpa liked the idea of the Rockin' Pig. We should have been off and running.

This trip, like many others, hit a snag before we were out the door. Once we had a plan, the kids (ages six through twelve) got antsy and fidgeted by the front door impatiently wanting to leave. Their parents went into "go mode" making sure they got the correct footwear from the pile and all went to the bathroom. Great Grandpa dawdled. He'd always think of some reason to sit awhile longer, asking, "What's the rush?" He'd tell someone to find him a pencil and paper so he could make a list or insist he wasn't finished with his coffee when only a sip had remained in his cup for the last hour. As usual, I was caught in the middle, trying to slow down the young families and hurry him up at the same time so we wouldn't get separated.

Parents and children piled into their respective vans. I managed to get Great Grandpa shoveled into his car along with his lady friend, Esther, Aunt Barbara and Uncle Mark. I had long since put my foot down about getting in a car if Great Grandpa was driving. His record wasn't great. He was a tailgater, impatient, and his reflexes had slowed to a crawl, but he still drove like an aggressive maniac, changing lanes, making sharp turns in front of other drivers, and not paying attention to signs. Greig and Marcia fell in behind us in their car.

There are two ways to get to Eureka Springs from Rogers. The families took off and I pulled out behind them, Greig bringing up the rear. Once on the highway, Great Grandpa said to me, "This isn't the right way to Eureka Springs."

I said, "The kids are going this way and I assume they're using GPS."

Great Grandpa said, "I don't need GPS; I know the way. I've lived here fifty years, been to Eureka Springs a hundred times. Stop the car and turn around. This is the wrong way."

I remained calm and controlled, and quite proud of myself. "Dad, I know there are two ways to get to Eureka Springs. I want to follow the kids so we all end up at the same place at the same time."

Great Grandpa wouldn't let up. "Stop the car!" he demanded. "This is my car and I'll drive."

Tensions rose, and I sensed a full-blown tirade coming. The three passengers in the back clammed up.

His license should have been taken away years ago. There was no way I would let him drive. Especially in this agitated state. All our lives depended on it.

"I'm not going to do that," I shot back with a look that could kill. "Just sit there and be quiet." Now I was the general. He did not like that. The hostility in the car was as thick as pea soup.

"Stop the car, I'm getting out," he said. I would have ignored him, but he was reaching for the door handle.

We were rounding a corner and there was an old building with an overgrown parking lot in front. I pulled into the parking lot thinking I would just let him out and drive off, as a lesson. Of course I would go back, but lucky for Great Grandpa, Greig pulled up next to our car and rolled his window down. "What's up?"

"Dad's complaining because we didn't take the highway he wanted to. I'm just following the kids. He wants out of the car and I'm done. Will you take him?"

"Sure." He pulled up so Great Grandpa could get out, and Marcia graciously got out of the front seat of their car and climbed in the back. Great Grandpa stomped over and took his place in the front, next to Greig. This was one of the things I liked about having Greig and his family at these reunions. Great Grandpa had always liked Greig. And Greig and Marcia were fond of Great Grandpa. They would always step up if I asked.

Without comment, Mark got out of the back seat of our car and moved to the passenger seat, and we all resumed the drive to the Rockin' Pig. In the meantime, the families had already scoped out a long length of picnic tables on the patio. Great Grandpa and Esther sat in the middle of the group, seats of honor reserved for them.

It was a beautiful sunny day, the setting perfect. The tension of the car ride was dissipating with pitchers of beer, or so I thought. The interior decor bespoke "biker bar" but outside it was just a regular patio, family-friendly, as advertised. We had it to ourselves. The kids could get up and run circles around us. Had we been surrounded by members of a Harley Davidson club it might've upset the ambiance but it didn't happen. We all ate "Wagyu" burgers, pizza, and drank sodas and beer and had a great time. No one but the people in on the drama of the ride to the pub knew anything had been amiss. Until, that is, the waitress came with the check.

"Ok, who's the lucky one?" She scanned the group. No one spoke. Everyone including her looked toward Great Grandpa. We all paused, respectfully giving him the opportunity for his big moment, waiting for him to say, "I'll take the check." But he didn't. Instead, he said, "I'll take a check for two, her (pointing to Esther) and me."

No one said anything. It took a moment for what had just happened to sink in. Then Greig and I and Keo jumped up and followed the waitress inside to have her recalculate the checks. Any one of us would have offered to pay in the beginning so there was no problem except that we'd all been taken by surprise. Only Greig and I and the passengers in our cars had a clue as to why Great Grandpa renigged on his previous insistent offer to buy lunch.

After lunch, we piled back into the cars, Great Grandpa rode with Greig and Marcia even though Esther rode in his car with me and Barbara and Mark. We continued the caravan to Eureka Springs. However, once there it became clear that Great Grandpa's mood had not eased because as soon as we parked and got out of the cars, he announced, "I want to go home. I'm taking my car. Give me the keys, Beth."

Staring daggers, I said calmly, "No, I'll drive you. The rest can stay and enjoy Eureka Springs." But everyone else decided it was fine to head home. I think when they saw the fiddlers on the corner and all the tourists lining the sidewalks, the gloss of Eureka Springs had worn off.

We went back to Great Grandpa's. He sat inside

steaming for a while. Esther stayed with him. The rest of us took drinks and snacks outside and set up the yard games Great Grandpa had provided. We played "corn hole", a popular bean bag toss game; ladder ball; and croquet in his great big back yard facing the thirteenth hole of the pristine Champions golf course. Beer, lemonade, comraderie, and competition suited us. After Esther went home, Great Grandpa came out onto his deck. Everyone soaked up fresh air and things returned to normal, well, normal for Great Grandpa's that is, where curveballs are common.

Karaoke singing. What can possibly go wrong?

GREAT GRANDPA AND THE KARAOKE MACHINE

I carefully extract my microphone from its plastic wrap and flick the "on" switch. Dead. Nothing. Can I just fake it? I wondered.

Ipaid a visit to Great Grandpa in the summer of 2018. His longest caregiver, Marlen, was taking a much-deserved vacation. I was to arrive two days after she had left. Everyone knew she would be gone for ten days. She generally worked four days a week and hardly ever asked for a day off, and even stayed the full week before with him because the other caregivers had abruptly quit. Only one other woman, Phyllis, had lasted more than a year with Great Grandpa. Phyllis might have been there to the end, alternating with Marlen, but she got cancer the year before and passed away within four months of her diagnosis. Although Great Grandpa had a heart, and expressed sympathy, he had a hard time forgiving Phyllis for dying. And he was resentful that Marlen was going away for ten whole days. He had told me she was being selfish to go for that long when he needed her.

This trip was important to Marlen. She could not change plans. There were others involved. But she dedicated the entire week before her trip, twenty-four-seven, to Great Grandpa. Staying past her usual days to train new caregivers. He had gone on a rampage and fired the other part time caregivers knowing that would leave him without any. He may have thought Marlen would then drop her plans and stay, rescue him. Marlen was the one that told me he fired them. Great Grandpa told me they had up and quit leaving him in a lurch. Over the course of the week that Marlen stayed, the agency sent over two new women for Marlen to train, the plan being each would stay part of the ten days. But neither would commit. A lot of caregivers had either been fired abruptly or stomped out leaving Great Grandpa with less than pleasant good-byes. He had a reputation at the agency.

When it came to caregivers, he was abrupt, very Donald Trump-esque about firing them. It was always their fault. He had a lot of complicated rules and rarely gave second chances, Some just couldn't take it. For example, caregivers were not allowed to use the sunroom door to the outside to water the plants and fill bird feeders even though it was much more convenient to get back inside to Great Grandpa if he needed something. The laundry room door at the other end of the house was for "the help" as he called them. It's true that they were all helpers, paid helpers, but Great Grandpa barked orders and talked about them within earshot disrespectfully. It seemed to me the weaker they were, the harder he was on them.

Another rule that drove me a little nuts – it applied equally to me - was about the dish washing sponge with liquid soap in it. If you laid it down, it leaked. That was grounds for firing. In order to keep it from leaking it had to be positioned upright in the sink at just the right angle. I found it to be a challenge because it kept slipping down into the sink. It was like putting a contact in your eye.

Some could do it easily, but I found it a source of frustration. I'd have just plopped it into a mug since it was really just about saving dish soap. But that was not allowed. If he wandered into the kitchen and found it leaking or in any position not according to the rules there'd be hell to pay.

And then there was the infernal bell. I call it that because it always felt like a demand. Lots of people would consider a bell a great help when caring for the elderly. Some elderlies would use a bedside bell judiciously. Great Grandpa's small antique bells which had short handles on them sat on side tables by each of his favorite chairs and by his bed. If he sensed a caregiver wasn't doing chores or fixing food for him, I'd see him pick up the bell. He'd tinkle it softly at first. If he didn't hear anyone say, "Coming, Mr. Maas (or "Mister Bill" as Marlen called him), he'd ring it louder. Ok, understandable. But then, if no one came he'd yell, "Where is everyone!" or shout "Marlen, where are you," making it seem like an emergency.

With a caregiver abruptly leaving and Marlen getting ready to go on vacation, he called me and said, "You need to come and take care of me while Marlen is gone, I can't get anyone else" I happened to be on a road trip heading toward Arkansas to visit him and could choose my arrival date. But I wasn't willing to dive into a shark tank. I knew if I showed up in the midst of the fray he would not try to get another caregiver and expect me to stay the ten days while Marlen was gone. My tolerance level was high, but not nearly that high.

"Can't do it, Dad. Let me know when you get a caregiver in place. I'll be a few days. I'll be happy to call the agency to get someone if you're having trouble. If they can't get someone in on short notice, there are other agencies."

I knew my limits. The infernal bell and barking out of orders didn't work for me. I brought too much baggage with me to Arkansas and Great Grandpa's superior attitude toward people that made it so he could stay in his home into his nineties was hard for me.

Since his only choice if he didn't get a new caregiver was to be alone, he called the agency. Collette arrived two days before me, and was trained by Marlen, on Great Grandpa's list of rules. Marlen had left an extra copy for me so I could help Collette keep from getting fired. I stopped in the first evening when I got to Rogers. Collette was very pleasant, all smiles. She was determined to please Great Grandpa and me. It gave me hope. But when she took me aside and confided in me that she had just left her husband and was basically homeless, I was elated yet troubled. Mean ex husband? Had to move out? A lot of questions came up in my head, but I didn't really want to know more about that. "TMI" (too much information} I thought, for the first encounter. Plus I knew Great Grandpa would not tolerate much of these secret conversations. I thanked her for being there, and accepted that she was a qualified caregiver, and maybe this was more serendipitous than cause for concern.

The next morning when I came to the house, something nagged at me. Collette seemed syrupy sweet, maybe a little too eager to please. After two days of being schooled by Marlen on the rules, I expected her to be a little more guarded.

We all chatted over coffee in the sunroom. Collette worked through the brainteaser exercises with Great

Grandpa, Then he picked up the newspaper and ceremoniously opened it, her signal to take care of the breakfast dishes and do some chores. It was a sunny day; she was sunny; I felt sunny too. Then it started. Collette had been with him only a few days and already she was on his grumble list. I had been checking the dish sponge so I knew it wasn't that. He began complaining about her, too loudly for my comfort. She was in the kitchen just on the other side of the wall. I tried to change the subject. He wouldn't have it. I listened to a bit of it, "She's not working out," he said, "she used the sunroom door when she knows she's supposed to use the laundry room door." and "She went out to water the plants when my bed needed to be made." Things like that, nitpicky. I shushed him and said we could talk about it later as she came around the corner with fresh coffee in hand and a donut on a plate for him.

There was no hint that she had heard him. We all chatted some more. She mentioned she liked to sing, and said she understood "Bill" (Great Grandpa) did too.

There it was, an opening. "How about some Karaoke", I said. "Dad has a machine."

"Really? Sounds like fun," Collette said.

"Marlen won't do karaoke," Great Grandpa complained.

"That's too bad," I said, thinking it maybe a bit unkind... But I also knew that Marlen was one of only two caregivers that had lasted longer than a year and it was because she was able to set reasonable boundaries of tolerance with Great Grandpa.

Karaoke sounded good to me, something we could do to fill time Great Grandpa might otherwise be difficult. His go-to for any gaps in conversation was to complain about someone. I had low tolerance for that and would much rather be doing something we all could enjoy.

Great Grandpa happened to have a karaoke machine from the days when he'd participated in karaoke sing-alongs at the church and Senior Center in Rogers with his friend, Elmer. He met Elmer through his other long-time caregiver Phyllis. Elmer was her brother. He had been a good friend, and he and his wife Joyce had also been part-time caregivers. Unfortunately, they were the ones that were fired or had quit the week before. It was Joyce, though, that was the catalyst. Great Grandpa detested Joyce as much as he loved Elmer. She acted sweet too, like Collette, but harbored bad feelings and sometimes complained to me quietly when she thought Great Grandpa out of earshot. Apparently, what lead up to the firing or quitting this time was that Joyce lost her cool. The end result was that she gave Great Grandpa a nasty parting denunciation of all of the reasons he was an ass.

With Marlen gone, and Joyce and Elmer gone, and Great Grandpa still smarting from Joyce's parting verbal assault, I wasn't sure how it would go with Colette. I was really pleased to hear that she liked to sing too. That was something they had in common.

Great Grandpa's karaoke machine proudly occupied prime real estate in his cluttered living room. He did love to sing and had a nice tenor voice, even though it was aging along with his tempo.

Since we'd done Karaoke at some of the five-year birthday party reunions, I knew what was coming next, a gauntlet of rules. One session had ended abruptly at a birthday reunion when two of the great grandchildren got a little carried away and usurped both microphones, singing and dancing, running circles around Great Grandpa. He shut it down demanding the microphones and chiding the group for being careless with expensive equipment.

We moved from the sunroom to the the living room, Great Grandpa picked up a package on his way and settling into his favorite chair, he held out microphones for Collette and I to take from his extended arms saying, "Don't open them yet." Once we were seated with our microphones, the instructions, were meted out, everything in order:

"First, unwrap the microphones … but be sure to save the bag. When not singing, …" and he emphasized these rules, "…be sure to turn off your microphone and put it back in the baggie …," explaining, "…darn kids always forget to turn them off. The batteries go dead."

This triggers a rant about things "kids" do that bug him. "Talk too fast … don't come visit enough … move his things so he can't find them … don't listen … don't follow directions … and on and on"

I carefully extract my microphone from its plastic wrap and flick the "on" switch. Dead. Nothing. *Can I just fake it?* I wondered.

Great Grandpa was barking out orders at Collette who was eagerly listening. She wanted to get things right. But there were a lot of rules. I knew it but I didn't think she did. I also didn't know if she knew Great Grandpa had a reputation at the agency for being hard on caregivers. He did not like change.

"It's impossible to train them," he'd complain. This was definitely a test for Collette and me. She was a puppet to Great Grandpa's manipulation of strings, awkwardly hustling to keep up.

"Turn the karaoke machine on first, ... no, I said turn the TV on first and then the karaoke machine ... not that button ... the other one ... down further ... not the machine, on the TV ... the higher switch above the low switch."

His voice was taking on an uncomfortable tone. It seemed he thought Collette wasn't listening. But I could see she was getting dizzy rotating in circles between the karaoke machine and the TV, which were ten feet apart.

I just observed, sitting with my dead microphone in my hand, waiting for some opportunity to casually mention that it wasn't working. I knew better than to interrupt the foray.

Finally, all the right switches were on, the karaoke machine was on, the TV was tuned into it, and song titles popped up. *Well, it's now or never,* I thought. "Uh, Dad, my microphone is dead." I winced.

"No, it's not!" He barked. "I know it's not, I just checked them recently."

"Sorry, dad, it is," I said as I got up and handed it over so he could see for himself.

"Damn kids." Great Grandpa hardly ever swore, in fact he didn't like people who did, but there it was.

Collette seemed relieved. The pressure was off of her, and on me. She had welcomed the idea of karaoke, happy to have something she could do with Great Grandpa "Bill" that would please him. And I liked her, she really seemed upbeat, but I could see her smile was tightening through the torrent of confusing instructions. I found myself holding my breath to see how she would cope. I had been so encouraged that she was in for the full ten day stay. But this was just her fourth day.

Great Grandpa's attention shifted back to Collette. "Colleen, get new batteries. They're in the kitchen drawer." Here's the thing. Her name is Collette and she'd corrected him about five times already just that morning. So had I. But he kept calling her Colleen and so we both finally gave up. It was clear he'd never call her Collette.

"Which one, Bill?" She said through pursed lips as she started toward the kitchen.

"Marlen was supposed to leave you instructions!" grumped Great Grandpa, pointing a bony finger toward the kitchen, "There, in the middle drawer."

I'm quite sure Collette was thinking the same thing I was, which was that there's no way Marlen could've thought of everything that might come up. But neither of us said that out loud.

Turning to look at me, for sympathy I guess, Great Grandpa complained, "I just can't get good help." He said it loud enough that Collette probably heard it through the open doorway to the kitchen. I sometimes wondered if he wanted the caregivers to hear him, to remind them who was boss. And I believed Marlen and Phyllis were able to tolerate it because they ignored him most of the time. But I wasn't sure about Collette yet. I desperately wanted her to work out, at least for the ten days Marlen was gone. I was afraid she would quit while I was there, and I'd be stuck with solving a big problem he created.

I prayed she wouldn't talk back to him because she definitely wouldn't last long if she did. Somehow, she managed to keep her cool as she retrieved batteries, and we all got our microphones working.

The index of songs ran bright white across the TV

screen. Great Grandpa and Collette liked Patsy Cline so we sang "I Fall to Pieces" and "Crazy" and some more oldies and had a very mellow singalong. I video'd us on my phone camera, played it back, and we all laughed. I prayed a little too and things went along fine for a while.

There were more rules I'd learned from the reunion karaoke sessions. And Collette seemed to have good enough instincts not to violate any.

Don't get too rambunctious.

Don't sing louder than Great Grandpa.

Do your best to try and find his beat, try to keep up, but don't get ahead of him at the awkward pauses.

Don't shake the microphone or dance around with it.

Don't be critical of oldies.

Don't ask for your music, even if he asks you what you want to sing.

And most importantly,

Do NOT sing along when Frank Sinatra's "My Way" comes up on the screen.

That song signals a grand finale.

If any of the rules are broken, the session will end abruptly. And for God's sake, be sure to turn off the microphone and stow it properly in its baggie when it's all over.

I left Arkansas on a high note this trip, contented that Great Grandpa would get the care he needed for the rest of the week. Collette had come two days before I arrived. And seemed to have what it took the three days I was there. But I got a call at 11:00 pm the day I left to drive back to California. I was at a motel seven hundred miles away. She was in tears, sobbing, "Bill insulted me. He's picking on me. I want to leave. I can't stand it anymore."

I did the best I could to calm her down. I could tell she wanted sympathy, wanted me to understand Great Grandpa was the problem. I already knew he was difficult, but felt she had some responsibility too, to her commitment. I reminded her she signed on for the full ten days, that she needed to ignore his insults, and that she had to stay until morning when she could call the agency to send a replacement before she could leave.

I could hear Great Grandpa picking at her in the background, so I asked to speak to him. I told him he'd be up shit creek and alone if he pushed her out the door, and that he should apologize. I felt like I was scolding two children and telling them to just get along. Holding both their feet to the fire was all I could do. I was half-way home and not turning around to go back to Arkansas.

A *special* lunch "for the boy". What can possibly go wrong?

GREAT GRANDPA
AND TWIN PEAKS

Noah froze. Great Grandpa handed his phone to Noah's dad, Keo, who was sitting across the table from him at the other end of the horseshoe, nodding to him to get ready to take the picture.

Keo, handed the phone back to Great Grandpa saying, "I don't think so, Bill."

Mid-morning after arriving one June in Arkansas to join me for a visit, my daughter Kristin, her husband Keo, and their two children, Noah and Kyla, came from their hotel to the house. Great Grandpa looked at the kids, and asked how old Noah was now. Noah said, "twelve."

Great Grandpa apparently assumed Noah had just turned twelve and before anyone could say anything else, announced, "I'll take you all to lunch, a special place, just for 'the boy'".

I might've seen a red flag had there been time to think because so many other times Great Grandpa had made a grand gesture to buy everyone lunch, things had gone awry, like the time of the Lake Tour, the Rockin' Pig, and lunches at Mimi's. But everyone was hungry and so we just blithely piled into two cars and followed Great

Grandpa's directions to the restaurant close his home called Twin Peaks. We all traipsed into the restaurant and Great Grandpa told the waitress there was a boy in the party with a birthday. It didn't matter that this was in June and Noah's birthday was December 22. No one said anything. I think we were all stupefied. A waitress walked up and asked, "How many?"

I was thinking *this girl sure has a skimpy outfit on.* She was young enough to be a teen, tiny in stature, and child-like in her short, I should say very short, denim skirt. A skimpy red bandana cotton triangular thing with a collar that you could hardly call a shirt was tied at her midriff. Her red cowboy boots and western hat with a red bandana hatband that matched the top completed the ensemble. And her pigtail braids with red bow ties really punctuated the look.

My eyes wandered away from our waitress and I saw all the young waitresses were similarly garbed. *This is the Arkansas version of Hooters,* I thought, ... stunned.

We formed a parade following the waitress, who led us to a large horseshoe shaped booth with bright red plastic sparkly seat and back upholstery and a copper tabletop. Noah scrambled in first toward the back of the booth, seeming to want to get as far away from the waitress as he could get. His mom and I flanked him. He seemed small, closing into himself. On the high end of the autism spectrum with Asperger's, he is extremely smart, but socially awkward at this age. He didn't like being touched by anyone he didn't know and trust. This came into play in a big way in Great Grandpa's next move.

Sitting at one end of the horseshoe booth, Great Grandpa was chatting with our waitress about something not related to food orders. He pulled his phone out of his shirt pocket while she stayed standing there, and began trying to coax Noah out of the sanctity of his safe spot between his bookends mother and grandmother saying, "We need to get a souvenir picture of this big day, me, and, looking directly at Noah, 'the boy', and Cindy [who was apparently the waitress]."

Noah froze. Great Grandpa handed his phone to Noah's dad, Keo, who was sitting across the table at the other end of the horseshoe, nodding to him to get ready to take a picture.

Noah's dad, Keo, handed the phone back to Great Grandpa saying, "I don't think so, Bill."

By now we were all, except for Great Grandpa, and maybe he was too, on the same page with the Twin Peaks – Hooters similarity. The waitresses were not as well endowed as the twenty-somethings of Hooters reputation; being instead nubile young flat chested girls, but the marketing motive was clear. And it was far from an appropriate choice for a twelve-year old boy, birthday or not. I am fairly certain we would left have at the pressure attempt of the photo op if we hadn't already ordered food.

We all exchanged eye-rolls as Great Grandpa apologized to the young waitress and dismissed her, oblivious to any sentiment among the rest of us. We were channeling our collective thoughts with looks, *Is he kidding? Twin Peaks? A special place for a 12-year old? Great Grandpa!!*

Noah was mature enough to be mortified long before we were. He didn't want to be the center of attention and certainly did not want to crawl out of the booth and get squished between Great Grandpa and this waitress person for a picture.

Great Grandpa wasn't done; he tried another tactic. He flipped through pictures on his phone and sent it around the table displaying a photo taken the time he was last at Twin Peaks. "Look, Sven liked having his picture taken," he said. There he was, all smiles, his arm around the shoulders of the little cowgirl waitress with a half-smile, eighteen-year old straight-laced Sven and his brand new girlfriend on the other side. Both Sven and the friend, whom he had not been dating long enough to call a girlfriend, looked strained, like their collars were too tight. But there were no collars on their T-shirts.

Great Grandpa sincerely believed this restaurant was perfect for a celebration of a twelve-year-old boy's birthday, and was taken aback that neither Noah nor anyone else was willing to get out of the booth and stand with him for a picture with the waitress. As for me, this was measuring up to be one more embarrassing fiasco.

We made it through the meal by speed eating, eyes on each other and our food and not Great Grandpa, out of respect for Noah's discomfort, which was palpable.

But just as we thought we were over the hump, things got worse. All the young waitresses headed in a wave toward our table bearing a mound of chocolate cake and ice cream with a candle in it and singing "Happy Birthday to Noah ...", and Noah, under his breath, had a quiet reply. I thought I heard, "[something indistinguishable... and then ... something unrepeatable ... and definitely] this is the most embarrassing day of my life."

When the meal was over, the cake, leaning candle, and puddle of ice cream was left untouched, out of character for this group. Normally such a treat would be devoured in minutes, or subjected to several competing spoons.

Instead we all scootched our way out of the sticky plastic booth, bare legs against plastic making little squeaks. Once free of the constraints of the booth, Noah bolted for the door like a circus jockey shot out of a canon.

Another 'memorable" lunch with Great Grandpa.

A list for gifting after death. What can possibly go wrong?

GREAT GRANDPA
AND THE LIST

*Jason was shy and looked uncomfortable being
the center of attention, his shiny shaved head
pinking up from embarrassment. We all stood
around to see which putter he would choose.*

During this five-year birthday in Arkansas, there was
a new twist to Great Grandpa's quest to get us to
show interest in his possessions. He had suffered more
than a few sarcastic remarks by my siblings and me about
having too much stuff, times ten. We would tell him it
could overtake him if he didn't get it under control. He
would tell us that we should turn his house into a museum after he died.

On the first day of one of these visits, he handed me
a List, three stapled pages with a blank to the left of
each named item. It was titled, "Distribution of Personal
Items, to be Given After Death". He asked me to have
each person put their initials in the box by by something
they liked. Then I was to write their name on a piece
of tape and stick it on the underside of the thing. This
was to identify who would get certain things when he
was gone. Since I was Trustee of his and my stepmother's
family trust, requests like this were not too far-fetched

Armed with The List, a roll of masking tape around
my wrist, and felt tip pen in hand, I circulated. There

were twenty of us. My two adult children and their kids and spouses were there. My sister Barbara and her husband Mark were there too, as well as my former husband, Greig, and his family. People were often surprised to hear that Greig and his second family were part of Great Grandpa's birthdays. But they liked Great Grandpa and the feeling was mutual. And I always made sure they were invited because, it took pressure off me. They were bona fide members of my buffer squad. And when there was a crowd around, Great Grandpa's demands on me to do things I thought unwarranted were minimized.

Great Grandpa's request was really a nonnegotiable directive, so I asked each adult to take a look at The List and identify what they wanted. After a while I could see there weren't going to be any takers. So I had to punt. Great Grandpa really wanted people to covet his stuff like he did. I could have said no, but it was his birthday. So, as a fitting gift, I pressed on, zeroing in on possible soft touches.

Jason, thirty something, was son-in-law to my ex-husband Greig, and I thought he might be talked into something. He seemed like a "Mikey" to me, the kid in the Life cereal commercials. "Let Mikey do it" was the catchphrase that came to mind. Mikey was the youngest in the commercial family, an easy patsy willing to try new cereal when none of the other boys would touch it. They all knew Mikey would try anything. Jason seemed the type. So I approached him.

"Jason, you're a golfer, may I put your initials by one of these golf clubs?" There were some putters on The List.

"Well I guess, sure, but I'm not really family."

"That's ok. Dad's stuff should go to someone who would like to have it."

He said, "Okay, I guess," and I put his initials n the box by a putter.

Then I went to my sister and begged her to find something she could claim. I told her it would make the birthday boy happy, so please do it. But the truth was, it would make me happy. I wanted to be done with The List. I didn't feel I could give up until I had at least some takers besides me.

"Barbara" I said, "you like antique furniture, what about the antique washstand."

She caved. "I guess so."

I had three takers, counting me and two others. *Enough*, I thought. I reported back to Great Grandpa. He took The List from me. However, instead of thanking me for my effort, he chose instead to single out the takers.

"Jason, come on with me and pick your putter." We all traipsed into the former dining room which was now a pool room, and gathered around the pool table. The walls were covered with large posters of Great Grandpa at all ages, in his naval flight uniform, with his golfing buddies at Pebble Beach Golf Course, outside the Grain and Feed Business he had owned in his thirties, and from his stint on the Board of the Iowa City Chamber of Commerce. Shelves and hooks affixed to the walls held colorful hats and visors from golf resorts all over the country. A large golf ball rack with about a hundred personalized golf balls was also affixed to a wall next to a rack holding about twenty pool cues and a few chalk blocks. There was also a shelf holding putters separated by wooden pegs near a tall thin umbrella can filled with a bouquet of other old golf clubs.

Jason was shy and looked uncomfortable being the center of attention, his shiny shaved head pinking up from embarrassment. We all stood around to see which putter he would choose.

"Just take any one of those putters," Great Grandpa said, pointing to the grouping of clubs on and against the wall.

Jason carefully plucked one off the rack and held it up toward Great Grandpa. "How about this one?" He seemed timid, but he was a golfer, so he had something in common with Great Grandpa. He and his wife Megan had been most excited of all of us that a prestigious Women's Invitational Pro Golf Tournament was taking place that week. They were recipients of two passes from Great Grandpa granting access to the galleries during the event. Security was tight so passes were required even in this gated community. In addition to the passes, they had front ro I was sure it was a coming to Jesus opportunity for them, since they lived in a small town in Iowa, far from any world class golf courses. I definitely felt Jason deserved a putter. But Great Grandpa hedged.

"Well, Jason, I don't think I'm quite ready to give that one up yet. But go ahead, pick another one."

"It's okay," Jason said, humbled, starting to back away.

"No, pick another one", Great Grandpa insisted. So, Jason chose another, and held it out tentatively.

"Hmmmmm," Great Grandpa said running his hand up and down the shaft of the club, "I'm not quite ready to give that one up either."

We all held our breath; but worried for naught. Jason was smart.

"Well Bill, thanks, I appreciate the offer. Would you like to choose one for me? I know I'm not family and not entitled, really, but if there is one you want to give to me, I would be happy to have it."

Now Great Grandpa was in a pickle. Jason's move was a good one. Then Great Grandpa lifted what looked like an old stick with a bump on the end out of the can and handed it to Jason.

"Here, take this one, in good health."

In unison, we all let out the breath we'd been holding.

Then, like the Pied Piper, Great Grandpa led the procession to the antique washstand in the living room. He turned to Barbara.

"Barbara, I see that you put your initials by the washstand. I will have Beth tape your name in the drawer. Since you are family, I would give you a good discount. What do you think you would be willing to pay for this antique washstand and pitcher set?

Taken off guard, she answered sarcastically, "Well, dad, I wasn't really intending to buy it."

Game over. Great Grandpa went straight to his recliner. picked up a newspaper and opened it wide, signaling the game was over. There was no further discussion of The List the entire weekend.

But Great Grandpa wasn't one to let go of things. Every time I visited after that, he would initiate at least one conversation with something like...

"You know, Beth, I really want to give away some of my things..."

"Okay, sure Dad," I would say, "just make a list."

Buying a new recliner. What can possibly go wrong?

GREAT GRANDPA
AND THE RECLINERS

*It wasn't even a week before he decided he
really did want a recliner lift chair and so he
asked Marlen to take him back to the store.
She put her foot down, "No, Mister Bill."*

Great Grandpa's collections were his friends. A stroll through his house was a tour through the past. The furniture and furnishings were original to the model home built in the eighties in the pristine community known as The Pinnacle Country Club. It is a private golf, tennis and social club in the rolling hills of Northwest Arkansas. Membership includes many of the wealthy Walmart heirs. It is advertised as a "family friendly" development but I never saw any families. To me, it appeared as an opulent development consisting of many castle-like monstrosities built by people with too much money. I always wondered just how many bathrooms and bedrooms one family needed. Since I hardly ever saw people around, I surmised many were probably second or third homes. When I walked about in the community to get fresh air and exercise, maintenance personnel were often out with gardening trucks or golf carts working on landscaping or the golf course, but I never saw anyone else out for a casual walk. In fact, there were no sidewalks, just cart paths and streets.

Great Grandpa's 2800 square foot, one story, three-bedroom model home, was a modest one by comparison to monoliths down the street from it. Its purpose as a model home was simple, to showcase the view of the long thirteenth hole on the championship golf course. Living in The Pinnacle, rubbing shoulders with golfers on a world-class golf course, enjoying an expansive view from his sunroom every morning with his coffee was a dream come true for Great Grandpa.

Mornings were always spent in the wicker rocker in the sunroom. But the rest of the day Great Grandpa was planted in the rocker recliner in the sunken living room. It didn't take long for anyone visiting to see that there were two chairs reserved for Great Grandpa, the rocker in the sunroom and the recliner by the lamp in the living room, and no one else sat in either of them.

The decoration in the model home was ahead of its time in the late eighties, but it already seemed dated by the time the New Millennium rolled over. Granted, to some, it may have appeared darkly rich. To me, some of the rooms were oppressive. The guest bathroom had no windows, was shrouded in dark blue and deep maroon wallpaper and an excessively poufy dark shower curtain, and felt like being in a cave.

Great Grandpa had filled the walls in the open rooms, hallways, and cluttered living with his collections. The atmosphere was heavy, especially in the later years as Great Grandpa lost mobility, became more sedentary.

When I visited, I wanted to spend as much time as I could in the brightest room in the house, the sunroom. We always had our morning coffee with light pouring in from the floor to ceiling windows. The plush green of the expansive back yard running right up against the golf course was a pleasant start to any day.

The sunken living room was for discussing business, like his trust, or for examining his coin collection, which were among our rituals. Great Grandpa would take up court in his blue-gray cloth rocker-recliner, me, in the matching one a few feet away. It was clear which chair was his. He'd have his caregiver stack all important papers and binders on side tables within his reach.

A lot of people fall in love with their recliner. They get it situated into just the spot, all things within reach and well positioned in order to watch TV. Luckily for Great Grandpa, the designers of the model home had identified just the right spot for his chair and it was not moved for more than thirty years.

Great Grandpa was self-centered and could be quite irritating. Sure, we all have character flaws, but as he got older, it seemed his most annoying traits were amplified. His temper got shorter, his disdain louder.

When I came to visit him in his advanced years, I noticed he was having some trouble getting out of his rocking recliner. The two blue ribbed cloth recliners in the living room were used every day. Eventually the lever on the "guest" rocker-recliner broke. So the footrest sloped off to the side if someone tried to recline. Great Grandpa's recliner could have had the same problem but it didn't really matter because there was a gigantic round glass table in the middle of the sunken living room stacked full of books and miscellaneous gifts he had received over the years that prevented reclining. There was no space for the footrests to pop up.

Great Grandpa's chair fit his body like a glove, a very

old, well-worn glove. When he got up you could see the dip in it. It was so deep he had to do some serious rocking back and forth to propel himself up and out. Both chairs were sadly sunken, just like the living room, and both eventually were fortified with flat seat and back pillows. Had it not been for that, one would sink to the floor.

When he reached his eighties, I first broached the subject, offering a gift of a recliner lift chair. I knew he'd never spend a penny on a stick of new furniture.

"Hey dad, you're getting up there, and your knees and back have been hurting, maybe you'd like a chair with some support. Maybe even a lift recliner. What do you think? We gave one to mom on her seventy-fifth birthday and she loves it."

My siblings and I had bought a recliner lift chair for our mother, otherwise known as Grandma Great, for her seventy-fifth birthday and it was her favorite gift ever. So naturally I thought Great Grandpa might like such a chair. Apparently offended by my light, albeit sarcastic attempt at a joke about his age, he came back at me emphatically, as if I was insulting him.

"No. I don't want a new chair. I like this one."

I dropped the subject like it was a hot potato that had just been tossed back to me.

A few years later, I talked to my siblings and we offered to get him a new recliner for his eighty-fifth birthday. Again, he said no thanks, again, that he didn't need it, that he liked his old chair. It was "broken in".

I brought it up a few more times as he approached ninety. It was becoming harder and harder for him to get out of his chair once he was plunked down in it.

His rote response was "No," always followed with

some pointed excuse.

"If I get a new chair, I'll miss the exercise I get from getting in and out of it. And my old chair is just fine, very comfortable. I can turn and rock and reach everything I need from it."

"Okay", I would say.

Then, on one of my visits, rather typical for him, having to be the one that came up with the ideas, he abruptly announced that it might be good to think about getting a new chair. I am guessing it was because the caregiver ladies were having a hard time getting him out of his chair.

So he and his caregiver Marlen went to The Recliner Store in Rogers. Sometime during the process of trying out chairs, he decided the young salesman was trying too hard to sell him something he didn't really want. He turned on a dime, offensively challenging the poor young man on the point that he did not need a lift recliner chair. He became so offensive in fact, that the manager was called over and Great Grandpa was kindly asked to leave the store. Marlen was mortified.

It wasn't even a week before he decided he really did want a recliner lift chair and so he asked Marlen to take him back to the store.

She put her foot down, "No, Mister Bill."

Great Grandpa told me afterwards on the phone that she was being unreasonable. I suggested he have a different caregiver call the store and have the chair he had tried and liked the most delivered. A new recliner was delivered shortly after that. He had it about a week and decided he didn't like it and wanted the store to come back and get it. But they wanted to charge for delivery and restocking. This made him really angry and so he called and was once again abusive, so awful they sent two men and a truck to take the chair back, no charge.

A few months later, Great Grandpa realized he really did need a new chair. He couldn't get down on the floor to do physical therapy but he could do the exercises in a chair that reclined to full-length. He could also nap in the chair and using the lift function could easily transfer to his wheelchair without being lifted up and out with a strap.

He announced that he wanted to go back and get the chair he had, but Marlen, a strong-willed fifty-year old Hispanic woman, refused to go back to the store or get involved in any effort to get him a new chair. She had lasted longer than any other caregiver, in large part because she could stand up to him, and she did on this.

Truth was he was having trouble getting caregivers to come to the house, let alone take him anywhere. He had quite a reputation at the Superior Senior Care Agency in Rogers. The owner worked hard to keep his business but some of the caregivers assigned to Great Grandpa had refused to go back a second time. Only the strong of character survived Great Grandpa. And Marlen was just that.

It didn't matter how much wheedling he did, she refused to get involved. Great Grandpa was stubborn, not about to go to a different store. And Marlen wasn't about to go back there. He and she had reached impasse.

The next time my sister Barbara and her husband, Mark, visited Great Grandpa, he told them he wanted to buy a lift recliner chair from The Recliner Store. Barbara knew the history, and she didn't really want to take him to the store. However, on this visit the weekend caregivers were present and they were a couple. Good buffers. Great

Grandpa liked the husband, Elmer, quite a bit. They had performed karaoke together at the senior center in town many times. He wasn't so pleased with the wife, Joyce, but he had to tolerate her since she was the agency's designated caregiver.

Barbara called me on the phone to commiserate. I said, "Why don't you and Mark take Elmer and Joyce to the store and make a party out of it. Great Grandpa will behave if Elmer's there. And surely the store is in the business of selling recliners and wouldn't turn down a sale even if it was to a grumpy old man."

They did all go to The Recliner Store and made it an afternoon of laughs, trying out different chairs and making up stories around Papa Bear's difficulties in choosing the right chair. Great Grandpa had to laugh along, since his friend Elmer was there, and somehow he ended up with three new recliners. He allowed my siblings and me to pay for the two matching rocking recliners for his living room since we'd offered to buy him a chair. He got his insurance carrier to pay for the zero-gravity lift recliner so he could do his physical therapy and nap in it. Everyone was happy, for a New York minute.

Euphoria was short lived however. I came for a visit soon after. I admired the new recliners, Before I got settled in he was grumbling that he really didn't want the new chairs, he wanted his old chair back.

"It's right there," I pointed to the two old recliners which were in plain sight in the raised dining room. They were sitting fifteen feet away in what had become the repository area for things that were no longer used, destined to be sold, with the player piano, piles of books, furniture and tables, and the pool table with its cues, racks, balls, and all things he could no longer use.

"I can bring your old chair right back in your spot right now if you like," I said, with a smile.

Clearly, he was just looking for an argument, not his old chair. But by now I had evolved into my just-be-agreeable phase, sometimes peppered with a pinch of sarcasm.

"No, don't move anything, I like my new chairs." He had turned my sarcastic offer back on me, using a scolding tone as if I was *threatening* instead of offering to bring his old chair back.

I was familiar with his game. Great Grandpa loved to stir the controversial pot. So I ignored the remark.

He wasn't done yet though.

He started complaining about the store manager. "The manager said they would take the old chairs if I wanted. I told him they should pay me for the chairs, but he wouldn't offer me a dime. In fact, he wanted me to *pay them* to take them away. Imagine, throwing away perfectly good chairs. They're worth a couple hundred dollars at least."

He tried to get me to agree the store manager was unreasonable. I was tempted to toss out a sarcastic comment, but I let it go. Great Grandpa could grovel and grump and grumble all he wanted about chairs.

I had a brand new comfortable chair to sit in when I visited. And I figured that now since there were three new recliners in the house, my siblings and I could sit around and roast Great Grandpa while he was looked down on us from his big recliner in the sky!

PART III

THE END

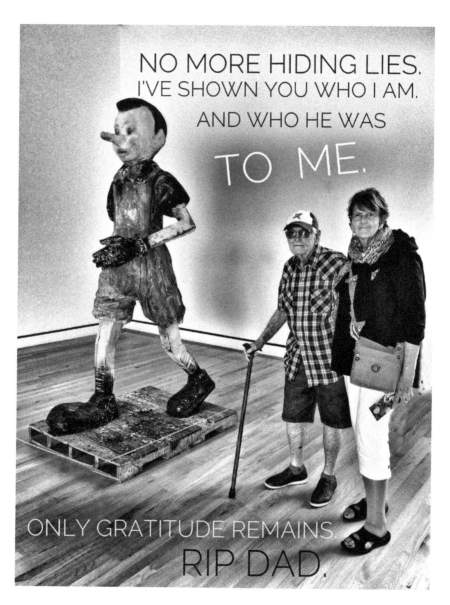

In the end, what sifted down and passed through the rubble was grace and gratitude. Not his, mine.

Writers are lucky. We can splay words on a page to express anger; pour emotions into cathartic essays; burn others in effigy; share burdens; entertain ourselves and others with stories, novels, or plays. We can use pens, pencils, paper, typewriters, and electronics that record our voices and memories to work through challenges, frustrations, or anything that threatens to put us over the edge, whether it be family dynamics, or dysfunctional behaviors on the part of others or ourselves.

And no one has to know, or everyone can know, depending on what the writer wants. With regard to my father, a man who most valued material things over relationships, I found writing to be a release valve.

I received a call from my brother Will on December 12, 2019, around ten pm, telling me our father had passed away. A heaviness lifted. Worries about what horrible fate might beset him as is raging behavior continued were over.

I had been in complete writers' block for over a month, stuck in the frenzy of his world. The ironic thing was that eight months earlier, I had pulled together a perfect plan to pull this collection of stories together into a book spending ten days in Kauai, Hawaii, for a writers' conference which would coincide with my birthday in November. I had thought this a perfect Trifecta. As I travelled to Hawaii, Dad's last chapter was just beginning. He was waging his final battle against death. My brother and sister and I had been in constant communication wondering what to do about his raging behavior. It was wreaking havoc in Arkansas. There was nothing lighthearted or funny about what was happening, and I couldn't even look at the stories I had written.

When he passed on December 12, he was finally at peace, and so was I. Freed from the source of a lifetime of subjugation, I could write again, and finish this book. I included this last part to share some extras that did not fit into any of the reunion stories, but that rounded out my own story of this relationship.

The Poem, "The Richest Ghost Town in America", was written at the airport on one of the days I was leaving Arkansas after a challenging visit. I ended up there nine hours before my flight was to leave, by choice. I had decided to try and spend a couple of extra days on this trip, in deference to him getting older and me always wondering if it would be the last visit. I knew full well that three days was about the max I could handle gracefully, but thought *what's the worst thing that can happen if I stay an extra few days?* I found out. The fourth day was rough. Five proved one too many. Early in the morning I told him I had to catch my plane at nine am when really it wasn't leaving until six pm. I couldn't be in his home another day. I found that the more agreeable I was, the harder he tried to pick a fight. By the fourth day it was ludicrous and exhausting. I don't like lying to people, but I wouldn't let him bring out my worst. I could've blown up, told him off, but to what end. As his caregiver drove him away from the terminal, I headed inside, but turned toward the car to wave goodbye. A passenger in his red Honda Accord, he slumped like the old man he was. It wasn't the first time I felt pity. I wanted to want to stay. I wanted to love him. But it wasn't in the cards.

Writing the Poem gave me an opportunity before I got back into my busy life to express my disdain for people and a place where materiality seems to come before relationships. I of course did not know what went on in any of the other houses in this opulent development but the absence of vibrance, of life in action, made it easy for me to assume there was something missing.

The other piece I included here is my goodbye letter. It was written on the morning after my father died. My brother Will was good at culling together celebrations. He requested something nice and positive to read at the memorial service. He was specific about that for a reason. There had been much underlying turbulence over the years. He needed to remind himself as much as reminding my sister and I that it was a memorial, not a roast. I did the best I could deciding on a gratitude list. By the time I was finished with the letter, I felt better. Some say you can forgive but not forget. Others say human memory leaves out some things in self-defense. I say gratitude lists are truly one of the best gifts to self. And it was a good time for it, I needed to give him a parting gift which would double as an apology of sorts, because I knew I had not been very forgiving of his behavior during last month of his life. I felt better after I finished my letter.

The saddest story in Waltonville. One more empty mansion.

THE RICHEST GHOST TOWN
IN AMERICA.

I call it Waltonville.
In the heart of Walmart country.

Ghosts everywhere
all around the neighborhoods
surrounding my father's house
next door neighbors on both sides
dead in recent years.
No one moved in
What is left behind?
gigantic vacant houses
well tended lawns and exteriors
no evidence of life.

My father seems as vacant as the houses.
Empty shell of a heart
running low on appreciation
soon to be severed from sustenance
his aortic valve closing by degrees
clogged by stress and greed.
And donuts.
With no defined end,
eventually the oxygen will cease to flow
his heart will stop beating
they tell it to him straight
nothing to do but wait,
live it out.

Fake plants gone greenish blue
in his sunroom and on his deck
where he spends his days
gazing at the empty fairways.

It's no better outside there in Waltonville
lifeless animals in coiffed yards
I pass by a deer in repose under a tree.
faded, chipped and lonely.

Little evidence of life in this vast wasteland of castles
lavish pools and empty chaises facing empty fairways.
But the saddest story I heard from my father
a young man with a family came into a large inheritance.
He built an excessive house on a small corner lot
stole the best view - overlooking a pond and fountain
became the subject of gossip at the club
a great faux pas in Waltonville
apparently.
He had worked and worked for a year
getting his castle just perfect
and then he died.
heart attack, at 47.
 I walked by the house on the corner lot many times.
No cars, no people, no light in the windows.
no sign of life.
A prime triangular plot of land.
bastion turrets reaching to the sky
ostentatious castle ... dream ... life ... gone.
What remains is a mammoth brick façade
a most elegant casket, another empty shell
in Waltonville.

For my 92 year-old father, it is just a matter of time.
A little or a lot, depending on how fast the days go by.
"Life" as it is in Waltonville,
he begs us all to come, spend more time,
wants to drive us around
to hear us ooh and aah at the castles.
He is very proud of this place
more proud than he is
of his three children.
and that is the saddest thing of all.

The chess set I brought home. As displayed in his
front entry hall with his other favorite things.

GOODBYE LETTER
AND FORGIVENESS

December 13, 2019 (The Day After My Father Died)
Letter to My Father

Dear Dad. It's time to say goodbye.

I'm sorry that I wasn't there when you passed away. I am sorry you suffered. I'm sure that even the shortest of winter days were long days for you, and the nights even longer, knowing you were dying.

I am glad you were surrounded by people that loved you and cared for you right up to the end, June, Lorena, Marlen. They were the ones that needed to be there, your angels. I was grateful for them.

I am at peace. I have finally followed my own advice and made a gratitude list about our relationship. It may have helped if I had done this earlier, but one can only move forward. You gave me some amazing gifts and good memories that deserve noting. Once I put pen to paper, I found there were more than I expected.

First and foremost, thank you for giving me strength and character. The strength came from the fortuitousness both you and mom exhibited during your lifetimes. Both she and you modeled that even when the chips are down one can pull themselves up by the bootstraps and move forward. Both of you instilled in me that I could do anything I wanted to do, that I would have many choices. This is a considerable gift. Admittedly the strength of character includes coping skills I learned in dealing with you and your resistance to recognizing me and other women in your life as being equals. Learning to cope with this taught me patience, acceptance, and forgiveness. We can't always get what we want, but we can always learn to love what we get. My only regret is that it took me so many years to figure this out.

And there were good memories.

I loved the road trips. Following Uncle Mac and Aunt Eleanor to the corners of the country, El Paso one year, Bangor, Maine the next, made the Christmas holidays a true adventure for me. I don't recall you ever paying tribute to your sister Eleanor in words, or hearing you say you loved her, but this did show you cared.

Maybe it was just wanderlust. That was the gift of the road trips for me. "Wanderlust". To this day, traveling, and especially paying tribute to the American highways and byways gets me across the country regularly. You did most if not all of the driving, sometimes in the most challenging conditions. I remember trips to Colorado and Wyoming and attending the World's Fair in New York, to this day. Sure, these trips were peppered with some speed bumps. Your treatment of mom could've been better. But I cherish the pictures you took of us three kids in front of road monument signs. I have done considerable traveling with my own kids and stopping for road sign pictures is part of our own repertoire because of this.

I enjoyed the trips to the turkey farm. My favorite thing was to ride on the water tanks to fill the turkey troughs. It felt like I was riding an elephant and the challenge was to hold on for dear life to the ring at the top of the tank. One of my favorite stories is when you taught me how to drive on a tractor. I dumped you off the back before you had a chance to tell me to let the clutch up slowly. To this day I remember you chasing the tractor through the open field yelling, "hit the brake, hit the brake!" I didn't know which pedal the brake was. It was a good thing the tractor was in low gear.

You taught me how to play golf and chess at a young age, before you distanced yourself from our family. Golf factored into my life in my twenties. At 25, I broke the country club record in Charles City, Iowa shortly after Greig and I moved there. As for chess, I taught my son Ryan and he taught his son Nathaniel to play. And the ceramic chess set I made you when I was in my twenties has a prominent place in my living room today, a cherished memento of a connection between us

I picked your brain about business, investing and real estate insight, seeking some things in common and my knowledge of these things helped me become a success. I was thankful we had these as topics on which to connect. And my life has been positively affected by this acumen.

And last but not least, without realizing it, your foibles gave me fodder for stories that helped me heal the most difficult relationship of my life, that with you. Unfortunately, I could not share the stories with you because you would not have enjoyed them. Being a man of appearance and outward charm, it wouldn't have occurred to you the absurdity of some of your actions and expectations could be humorous.

You were my most peculiar muse.

The Great Grandpa Chronicles will soon come to print, a collection of stories gathered from the reunions, and my visits to Arkansas, and my own journey from ambivalence to acceptance.

I have many things to be thankful for in memoriam. Most of all I am thankful your suffering is over. I hope that you have received the gift of redemption from any pain you may have caused or suffered, and that in passing through the pearly gates, you pick up a good sense of humor so you can appreciate the voice in **The Great Grandpa Chronicles.** Lest you think I am picking on you, You're not alone. Looking for the humorous things people do in difficult situations is a great coping mechanism. When I am gone my only hope is that my own children will remember my life through rose colored glasses that enable them to appreciate the best of me, and remember things that made them laugh.

So, Dad, it's time to say goodbye ... for now.

I found myself on a peaceful plateau of acceptance,
of him and of myself.

AFTERWORD ...
MY FATHER, MYSELF

I had reached a pinnacle in navigating a truly dicey relationship. And I found myself near journey's end, on a peaceful plateau of acceptance, of him and of myself.

Did you ever hold onto contempt tightly for someone most of their life, only to end up giving in easily after they die? And then wonder why you couldn't let go earlier?

So many questions. That's the way of it with my father. He was such a challenge for me. This is my story, how I saw him and how it affected my life. I believe he was essentially a happy man, oblivious to anyone else's feelings or expectations. He walked life on the surface, selfishly grabbed up what he could, seldom gave without motive or expectation of return. That must be an easy way to live.

My entire life has been affected by his narcissistic behavior. I simply wanted more than he could give, and didn't have time to figure this out until late in my life when I could finally write about it. I wanted to be a good person, and it seems that should mean being a good daughter too. So, as much as his behavior toward me and other women frustrated me, I just kept trying to do things that would elicit his appreciation. A lot of what

I did fell flat until I became a lawyer, someone of status to him. I didn't do it to please him, but I might have done it to spite him. And instead of accepting that he was proud of my achievement, I resented him for it.

What a merry-go-round we were on. I learned a lot from him, but I believe even these things were borne of my need to connect. I soaked up knowledge he had of golf, real estate, business, and investing. Throughout my life these interests provided a common thread. Having a daughter was not enough for him. And no amount of savvy he held replaced a daughter's need to be loved.

That left me with a nagging malady that affected me in all male relationships. I wouldn't stay with anyone who did not fully appreciate me for who I am.

This book morphed into a much different form than first anticipated. It started out as a collection of humorous stories about my father, hence, the title, "The Great Grandpa Chronicles". But it ended up to be more of a chronicle of my own ragged journey from one side of a great relationship challenge to the other. And I didn't even realize that it was happening until the end, when it was time to pull it all together into a book.

When we were young, if we complained or accused our father of not loving us, he would say, "I don't need you to love me, I need you to respect me." I hated that phrase. But now, …God, how I did not want to respect anything about him! But I couldn't help it. He didn't know how to treat women as they should be treated, but he was not a bad man. It took me understanding my father to fully understand myself. Through coping with his resistance to honoring me, I found that I was capable of all things, tolerance, understanding, resilience, patience, wisdom, and strength. And indeed, I had learned these things by damaged example.

And when all was said and done, and written, I found I could appreciate him.

Writing was the key to understanding my father and myself. I identified the ambivalence mid life and at that point was done purging. I skated through the stories, and laughed. I saw him through the eyes of my grandchildren, and graced him with acceptance, blessed him, and said good-bye on the best possible terms.

Lightning Source UK Ltd.
Milton Keynes UK
UKHW021601151220
375260UK00006B/81